THE UNOFFICIAL GUIDE TO
BASEBALL'S MOST UNUSUAL RECORDS

BOB MACKIN

THE **UNOFFICIAL** GUIDE TO

BASEBALL'S

~ MOST ~

UNUSUAL

RECORDS

GREYSTONE BOOKS

DOUGLAS & McINTYRE PUBLISHING GROUP

VANCOUVER/TORONTO/BERKELEY

For Sherry, my mother.

Copyright © 2004 by Bob Mackin
04 05 06 07 08   5 4 3 2 1

Greystone Books
A division of Douglas & McIntyre Ltd.
2323 Quebec Street, Suite 201
Vancouver, British Columbia
Canada V5T 4S7
www.greystonebooks.com

National Library of Canada Cataloguing in Publication Data
Mackin, Bob, 1970–
    The unofficial guide to baseball's most unusual records / Bob Mackin.
    Includes index.
    ISBN 1-55365-038-7
    1. Baseball—Miscellanea. I. Title.
GV873.M32 2004   796.357   C2004-900060-8

Library of Congress information is available upon request.

Editing by Anne Rose
Cover and interior design by Jessica Sullivan
Cover photo by AP/Wide World Photos
Typeset by Tanya Lloyd Kyi
Printed and bound in Canada by Friesens
Printed on acid-free paper
Distributed in the U.S. by Publishers Group West

We gratefully acknowledge the financial support of the Canada Council for the Arts, the British Columbia Arts Council, and the Government of Canada through the Book Publishing Industry Development Program (BPIDP) for our publishing activities.

Vancouver's BOB MACKIN is an award-winning sports journalist who fell in love with baseball watching the Vancouver Canadians of the Pacific Coast League, from their birth in 1978 to their 1999 PCL championship season. *The Unofficial Guide to Baseball's Most Unusual Records* is his fourth title (and third baseball trivia book) for Greystone. Mackin also covers music, politics, government, business, outdoor recreation and travel for newspapers and magazines across Canada and the U.S. The author welcomes comments and suggestions via e-mail to *offthewallbaseball@hotmail.com*.

Contents

Introduction

People often ask why I love baseball. The answer is simple: all the unusual people who are drawn to the game.

Jack McKeon is one such character. I first interviewed Jack in 2002, some 40 years after he managed my hometown Vancouver Mounties. I contacted Jack to learn about that day in July 1962, when he made baseball history by attaching a one-way radio to the inside of pitcher George Bamberger's jersey. McKeon was only too happy to talk about the incident, even though he was enjoying his retirement. Only a year later, at age 72, Jack was leading the Florida Marlins to a World Series championship.

Although it's thrilling to see players—and would-be retirees— change the game, I also sit on the edge of my seat every summer just to see what Mike Veeck has up his sleeve. Since his infamous anti-disco rally at Chicago's Comiskey Park in 1979, the son of baseball's own P.T. Barnum, Bill Veeck, has revolutionized minor league baseball with ridiculous, but sublime, fan-pleasing promotions—all in a bid to put bums in seats. Last year, for example, one of Mike's teams held a Silent Night at the ballpark; a year earlier, he set a no-attendance record with nobody in the grandstands.

Then there's the San Diego Chicken, Ted Giannoulas. Hatched in Canada but raised in San Diego and schooled at Ted Williams's alma mater, Hoover High School, Giannoulas crisscrossed the continent for more than a quarter-century as baseball's top grossing mascot. And what about Max Patkin? The late, great rubber-faced clown prince of baseball, who had a bit part in the film *Bull Durham*, didn't need a mask to bring mirth to ballparks big and small. Why doesn't someone make a movie about *him*?

Still, my favourite baseball character of all time is Bill Lee—the infamous "Spaceman." Always laughing in the face of authority, the Boston Red Sox and Montreal Expos pitching great makes a living these days by barnstorming. He was always an oddity off the mound, practising yoga and eating health food—even confessing to sprinkling marijuana on his pancakes. When I spoke with him in 2002, he told me he was planning on running for President of the United States of America in 2004. Imagine that: Bill Lee campaigning against a former owner of the Texas Rangers, George W. Bush.

Now, wouldn't that be unusual?

BOB MACKIN
January 2004

CHAPTER 1

Play Ball!

GETTING STARTED

Joe DiMaggio hit safely in 56 consecutive games. Pete Rose amassed 4,256 hits in his career and Barry Bonds blasted 73 home runs in a season. Cal Ripken Jr. played 2,632 games in a row. The records are different, but each player started on his journey to greatness the same way, on hearing the two most magical words in sports: "Play ball!"

Most leadoff home runs in a career

81: Rickey Henderson

How's this for starting with a bang? When the game's greatest leadoff slugger—Chicago native Rickey Henderson—joined the Los Angeles Dodgers (his ninth team in 25 seasons), he broke his own record for leadoff home runs. In only his third start in Dodger blue on July 20, 2003, Henderson slapped a Woody Williams pitch out of Dodger Stadium for his 81st game-starting home run. The Cardinals, however, were 10–7 winners. (Henderson started his major league career with the Oakland Athletics in 1979, and helped them sweep the 1989 World Series with a leadoff dinger in Game 4.)

Most consecutive home runs to start a game

3: Rafael Furcal, Mark DeRosa and Gary Sheffield, Atlanta,
  May 28, 2003
3: Marvell Wynne, Tony Gwynn and John Kruk, San Diego,
  April 13, 1987

Jeff Austin could have sprained his neck when he started for the Cincinnati Reds in Atlanta on May 28, 2003. Why? He kept turning around to watch his pitches sail over the outfield fence. It happened three consecutive times in the Braves' 15–3 win. Atlanta shortstop Rafael Furcal, second baseman Mark DeRosa and rightfielder Gary Sheffield registered the solo shots. Austin wasn't pulled from the game until Javy Lopez added a two-out, two-run homer. The four round-trippers traveled 1,585 feet. Wynne, Gwynn and Kruk sounds like a law firm, but these are the names of the San Diego Padre outfielders who homered in back-to-back-to-back style to start a 1987 game. Centerfielder Marvell Wynne, rightfielder Tony Gwynn and leftfielder John Kruk connected consecutively to begin the 13–6 home loss to the San Francisco Giants.

Only player to hit home runs in first two at-bats

Bob Nieman, St. Louis (AL), September 14, 1951

Baseball fans mentioned Bob Nieman's name in the same sentence as Babe Ruth for all of one day. That day was in 1951, when a St. Louis Browns rookie began his career with two consecutive home-run blasts. Boston Red Sox pitcher Mickey McDermott allowed the homers, but Boston withstood Nieman's onslaught as Dom DiMaggio, Ted Williams and Walt Dropo countered with four-baggers in the 9–6 win. Nieman went on to play 12 years and add another 123 home runs to his docket; he finished 630 behind Ruth on the all-time list.

First player to hit a home run as a pinch-hitter in first major league at-bat

Chuck Tanner, Milwaukee, April 12, 1955

Chuck Tanner had a pinch of beginner's luck when he strode to the plate for the first time of his career in the eighth inning of a 1955 game. The Milwaukee Brave hit a home run off Gerry Staley to help beat the Cincinnati Reds 4–2. Tanner lasted seven years in the majors as a player, but came back and managed for 19.

Fastest managerial resignation

1 game: Eddie Sawyer, Philadelphia, April 14, 1960

Here today, gone today. It took just one loss for Eddie Sawyer to decide he had had enough of managing the Philadelphia Phillies. The 9–4 Opening Day loss to the Cincinnati Reds was the last game he ever managed and the first of 95 defeats for the National League's last-place team in 1960. Sawyer spent his entire managerial career with the Phillies. He was fired in 1952 after five seasons, but returned in 1958 for a second go-round. He called it quits just 10 wins shy of 400.

First baseball game played under artificial lights

Jordan Marsh vs. R.H. White, Hull, Massachusetts,
September 2, 1880

Attention shoppers! When department-store-sponsored teams Jordan Marsh and R.H. White met at Nantasket Beach Sea Foam House on September 2, 1880, it was an illuminating ball game — the first with "electric sunshine." Northern Electric Light Co. provided two engines and three generators to power 36 lamps on three wooden towers. The teams tied 16–16. Another 55 years went by before Major League Baseball began play under the lights.

First radio broadcast of a major league game

Philadelphia at Pittsburgh, August 5, 1921

In 1921, you didn't have to "turn up" at a game in Pittsburgh. All you had to do was tune in with Pittsburgh radio station KDKA, the first to broadcast a major league game. Harold Arlin, a 26-year-old who worked for Westinghouse by day and KDKA at night, handled play-by-play duties. He didn't have to talk for long, as the host Pittsburgh Pirates beat the Philadelphia Phillies 8–5 in a quick hour-and-57-minute game at Forbes Field, where Arlin sat in a field-level box seat to describe the game for listeners. (Arlin's grandson, Steve, would become a major league pitcher: he was 34–67 with the San Diego Padres and Cleveland Indians from 1969 to 1974.)

First major league batter seen on TV

Billy Werber, Cincinnati, August 26, 1939

Billy Werber, you're a star! The Cincinnati Reds third baseman made television history just by leading off against the Brooklyn Dodgers at Ebbets Field in the first televised major league game on NBC's New York TV station, W2XBS. Legendary Dodgers game-caller Red Barber was behind the microphone for the doubleheader. The Reds won the opener 5–2 and the Dodgers responded with a 6–1 win for the split.

Only Opening Day forfeit
New York (NL) vs. Philadelphia (NL), April 11, 1907
Catcher Roger Bresnahan was all dressed up with no place to play when the 1907 season opened. He came to New York's Polo Grounds wearing cricket pads to protect his legs, but the weather did not cooperate. Snow was removed from the field before the game, though just enough remained for rowdy New York Giants fans to make snowballs. Without police to restore order, umpire Bill Klem awarded the Phillies a 9–0 forfeit win.

First regular-season game between American League and National League clubs
San Francisco vs. Texas, June 12, 1997
The cynics among Texas Rangers fans thought they would never live to see their team play a meaningful game against a National League team. But when it finally happened in 1997, it wasn't what they had wished for. The Rangers hosted the San Francisco Giants in Major League Baseball's first regular-season showdown between teams from opposing leagues. The Giants edged Texas 4–3 to open the era of interleague play. It was really a ploy by franchise owners desperate to reverse an attendance slump. But the players' strike that cancelled 1994's World Series continued to hurt teams at the gate. Until interleague play, the only way for National and American League teams to meet for keeps was in the World Series.

Most home runs on Opening Day

3: George Bell, Toronto, 1988
3: Karl "Tuffy" Rhodes, Chicago (NL), 1994
George Bell hit a trio of dingers for the Toronto Blue Jays
to kick off the 1988 season on April 4. Bell rounded the
bases in the second, fourth and eighth innings off Bret
Saberhagen of the Kansas City Royals. The Blue Jays won
5–3. Karl "Tuffy" Rhodes notched his Opening Day hat
trick on April 8, 1994, when the Chicago Cubs beat the
New York Mets 12–9.

Only players to lead off both games of a doubleheader with a home run

Harry Hooper, Boston, 1913; Rickey Henderson, Oakland, 1993
Boston Red Sox fans experienced *déjà vu* on May 30, 1913, when
outfielder Harry Hooper began both halves of a doubleheader
against the Washington Senators with a home run. The Senators
won the opener 4–3, but the Red Sox took the second 1–0 on
Hooper's homer. Rickey Henderson matched Hooper's feat on
July 5, 1993—for the Oakland Athletics in a doubleheader with the
Cleveland Indians. The A's won the first 6–5, then lost 6–2 for a split.

Most home runs in the first 10 days of a career

6: Dino Restelli, Pittsburgh, 1949
They say there is no rest for the wicked, but Dino Restelli was
wicked to the pitchers he faced during his first week and a half in
the big leagues. The Pittsburgh Pirates outfielder registered six
home runs in the first 10 days of his career in June 1949. Despite his
meteoric start, however, Restelli homered only three more times in
a major league career that featured 93 games in two seasons.

Worst self-inflicted injury at home plate in first major league at-bat

Billy Herman, August 29, 1931

Billy Herman's first major league at-bat was a real headache. In his first trip to the plate in 1931, the Chicago Cubs second baseman swung at Cincinnati Reds pitcher Si Johnson's offering and hit the ball, which then ricocheted off the back of home plate and struck him in the back of the head. Herman was knocked out cold, but at least the Cubs were 14–5 winners.

Only player to play with the same team in three cities

Eddie Mathews, Boston, Milwaukee and Atlanta

Mathews was a rolling stone. Wherever the Braves went was his home. First Boston, then Milwaukee and finally Atlanta — Mathews was the only player to don the team's colors in all three cities. The third baseman began his career in 1952 in Boston, then played the club's entire 1953–1965 stay in Milwaukee before following them south to Atlanta in 1966. He finished his career a Detroit Tiger in 1968, and was inducted into the Hall of Fame 10 years later, wearing a Milwaukee cap on his plaque.

Only athlete to play for three professional sport franchises in the same city

Gene Conley, Boston, Celtics, Braves and Red Sox

He's Gene, Gene, the championship ring machine! Gene Conley won three National Basketball Association championship rings and another ring in the World Series. The six-foot-eight pitcher earned his only big-league championship with the 1957 Milwaukee Braves, though he began his baseball career with the 1952 Boston Braves. The Braves — who paid him $1,000 to stop playing basketball — traded Conley to the Philadelphia Phillies in 1959. He later quit baseball and returned to Boston, where he helped the Celtics win the NBA title for three straight seasons. Conley resumed his baseball career in 1961 with the Boston Red Sox, but failed to lift them into the World Series before he retired in 1963.

First player drafted
Rick Monday
A Tuesday was the greatest day in the life of a young Rick Monday, when, on June 8, 1965, he was the first player chosen in Major League Baseball's first amateur draft. Monday, an Arizona State University sophomore, signed with the Kansas City Athletics for a $104,000 bonus before making his debut on September 3, 1966. He continued his 19-year career with the A's in Oakland, then joined the Chicago Cubs and Los Angeles Dodgers.

First major league ballplayer born on February 29
Dickey Pearce
Some would say that shortstop Dickey Pearce's birthday came only once every four years. For Pearce, born in 1836, was baseball's first "leap year baby." Others include: Ed Appleton (1892); Ralph Joseph Miller (1896); Roy Parker (1896); Pepper Martin (1904); Al Rosen (1924); Paul Giel (1932); Steve Mingori (1944); Al Autry (1952); Jerry Fry (1956); Bill Long (1960); Terrence Long (1976).

First player to get a hit for two teams on the same day in two separate games
Joel Youngblood, New York (NL) and Montreal, August 4, 1982
Joel Youngblood made an impression in his last game for the New York Mets and his first game with the Montreal Expos—all on the same day in 1982. Youngblood recorded a two-run, third-inning single for the Mets against the Cubs in a 7–4 win of a day-contest at Wrigley Field, Chicago, before being dispatched to the Expos, who were playing in Philadelphia. Youngblood traveled to

Philadelphia and singled off pitcher Steve Carlton, but the Expos were 5–4 losers.

Only Opening Day no-hitter
Bob Feller, Cleveland, April 16, 1940
Chicago White Sox fans waited from the fall of 1939 until the spring of 1940 to see their team hit a ball in Comiskey Park. They had to wait an extra day, too, thanks to Cleveland Indians pitcher Bob Feller. On April 16, 1940, Feller ruined the Sox home opener with a 1–0 no-hit gem in the Windy City. It was the first of Feller's three career no-hitters.

Most hits in a one-game career
4: Ray Jansen, St. Louis (AL), September 30, 1910
Ray Jansen of the St. Louis Browns had a career game in 1910 — the key words being *career game*. It was the only time the St. Louis native played in the majors, and he went 4-for-5 at the plate in a 9–1 loss to the Chicago White Sox.

First African-American on a baseball card
Jimmy Claxton, Oakland (PCL), 1916
Every picture tells a story, and the one of Jimmy Claxton on a Pacific Coast League baseball card is bittersweet. During practice, a Zeenut Company photographer snapped a shot of the Canadian-born Claxton in action. On May 28, 1916, Claxton went 2⅓ innings with the Oakland Oaks in a doubleheader, yielding four hits, three runs and four walks in his only action. Claxton, who had always dreamed of playing baseball professionally, had joined the team under the ruse that he was a native Indian and was released when management found out he was Afro-American. But such considerations didn't matter to Zeenut, which issued the first baseball card featuring a black player.

CHAPTER 2

The Delivery

PITCHING PECULIARITIES

Every play begins in the mitt and in the mind of the pitcher, the only resident of the 18-foot circular island called the mound. In fact, pitchers are the only players in any field sport who are on higher ground—a whole 10 inches more than their teammates and competitors. Sometimes, pitchers also elevate their performances beyond expectations. Other times, they sink to new lows.

Most innings pitched in a game

26: Joe Oeschger, Boston (NL), and Leon Cadore, Brooklyn (NL), May 1, 1920

Boston Brave Joe Oeschger and Brooklyn Robin Leon Cadore both worked overtime on May 1, 1920, but neither one took care of business by tossing 26 innings each for their respective teams. The game ended in a 1–1 tie. Neither pitcher allowed a run during the final 20 innings of the game, which lasted a relatively quick three hours and 50 minutes at Braves Field in Boston.

Most consecutive pitching wins

24: Carl Hubbell, New York (NL)

If you were a New York Giants fan in 1936 and 1937, you had complete confidence in Carl Hubbell. He was so reliable on the mound that he earned the nickname "Meal Ticket." Hubbell also compiled a winning streak that lasted two-dozen games. The streak began July 17, 1936, and continued until May 27, 1937. Hubbell's first 16 wins were in 1936.

Most consecutive wins in a single season

19: Rube Marquard, New York (NL)

Rube Marquard was dubbed the "$11,000 Lemon" after he scored a record contract but failed to meet expectations early in his career. By his fifth season, however, the future Hall of Famer had the Midas touch. In 1912, he pitched 19 consecutive wins for the New York Giants — a streak that ended at Wrigley Field in Chicago when the Chicago Cubs beat the Giants 7–2 and dealt Marquard his first loss of the season. He finished the season in a slump with seven wins and 11 losses for a 26–11 record.

Most pitching triple crowns

4: Grover Cleveland Alexander

It's good to be the king. Philadelphia Phillies ace Grover Cleveland Alexander had 31 wins, 241 strikeouts and a 1.22 ERA in 1915 to claim his first of three consecutive National League pitching triple crowns. In 1920, he won a record fourth with the Chicago Cubs.

Most consecutive pitching losses

27: Anthony Young, New York (NL)

His name was Young, but his losing streak was too "old" for a franchise all too familiar with the agony of defeat. In 1993, Anthony Young lost 27 games in a row for the New York Mets. The slump dated back to 1992, when Young last won on April 19—an 11–6 decision over the Montreal Expos. To set the futility record, Young walked home the winning Los Angeles Dodgers run on July 24, 1993, in a 5–4 10-inning game.

First pitcher to win 20 games, then lose 20 the next season

Joe McGinnity, Brooklyn, 1900

Joe McGinnity had 20/20 vision, though you could say it was 29/20. For McGinnity led the Brooklyn Superbas in 1900 with a 29–9 record and went 26–20 in 1901 with the Baltimore Orioles. "Iron Joe," who pitched professionally until he was 54, won 247 games over 10 big-league seasons and lost 144.

Most 20-game winners

4: Chicago White Sox, 1920
4: Baltimore Orioles, 1971

One pitcher with 20 wins is good for any pitching staff. But four? That's extraordinary. Only twice in baseball history have teams had so many pitchers at or above the 20-win threshold. The 1920

Chicago White Sox featured 23-game winner Red Faber and 22-game winner Lefty Williams. Eddie Cicotte and Dickie Kerr added 21 wins apiece. Yet despite their pitching strength, the White Sox finished second—two games behind the Indians. Not until the 1971 Baltimore Orioles did another lineup feature such a quartet: Dave McNally led with 21, while Pat Dobson, Mike Cuellar and Jim Palmer had 20 each. The Orioles won the American League pennant, but lost the World Series in seven games to Pittsburgh.

Most career losses without a victory

16: Terry Felton, Minnesota

When Minnesota Twins pitcher Terry Felton was granted three wishes, he forgot to ask for a major league victory. Felton set a record for most losses without a win when he had his 15th futile appearance on August 15, 1983. He was in unfamiliar territory that game with a no-hitter for five innings against the Seattle Mariners. Then came the sixth when he was charged with four runs. Felton finished his career at a dismal 0–16.

Worst single-game pitching performance

Doc Parker, Cincinnati, June 21, 1901

Cincinnati Reds pitcher Doc Parker could have used a real "doc" on June 21, 1901, when he let the Brooklyn Superbas run amok with 26 hits in Cincinnati's 21–3 loss.

Only team since 1900 to be out-won by a pitcher

Washington Senators, 1904

The 1904 Washington Senators needed help. Perhaps pitcher Jack Chesbro was all they needed, but he already belonged to the New York Highlanders. The Senators were a dismal 38–113. Chesbro won an American League-leading 41 games, three more than the entire Senators staff.

First pitcher to win two complete games in one day

Joe McGinnity, New York (NL), August 1, 1903

They didn't call New York's Joe McGinnity "Iron Joe" for nothing. To begin August 1903, he worked both ends of a Giants doubleheader to beat Boston 4–1 and 5–2.

First doubleheader shutout

Harry Staley and Pud Galvin, Pittsburgh, April 13, 1888

The Boston Beaneaters were speechless after losing a doubleheader without even scoring a run. It happened on April 13, 1888, at the hands of the Pittsburgh Alleghenys. Pitchers Harry Staley and Pud Galvin were credited with the respective 4–0 and 6–0 wins in the twinbill.

Most shutouts in a day

2: Ed Reulbach, Chicago (NL), September 26, 1908

Chicago Cubs pitcher Ed Reulbach was superb and the Brooklyn Superbas were not during a 1908 doubleheader. Reulbach pitched the Cubs to a 5–0 and 3–0 shutout sweep.

First pitcher to record a shutout in first start

Albert Spalding, Chicago (NL), April 25, 1876

Albert Spalding of the Chicago White Stockings blanked the Louisville Grays 4–0 on April 25, 1876, earning the first shutout by a pitcher in his first start. How did he follow it up? Two days later, Chicago beat Louisville again, this time with a 10–0 score.

Most consecutive scoreless innings

59: Orel Hershiser, Los Angeles, 1988

It took one more retired batter to push Orel Hershiser ahead of another Los Angeles Dodgers great to set the record for most consecutive scoreless innings. Hershiser's 59 straight blank innings in 1988 edged Don Drysdale's 58⅔ from 1968.

Most saves in a season

57: Bobby Thigpen, Chicago (AL), 1990
They should have called him Bobby "Bullpen," because that's where Bobby Thigpen could be found whenever his Chicago White Sox needed to finish a game they were winning. Thigpen collected 57 saves during the 1990 season with the White Sox, the only year he played in an All-Star game.

Most consecutive saves

63: Eric Gagne, Los Angeles, 2002–2003
Los Angeles Dodgers fans spelled relief G-A-G-N-E in 2002 and 2003, as relief pitcher Eric Gagne compiled a 63-game string of saves from August 28, 2002, through September 24, 2003. Gagne's only blown save in 2003 was for the National League in the All-Star game, but that didn't count in regular-season standings. The Montreal native was voted the National League's Cy Young Award winner in 2003.

Longest relief assignment

18⅓ innings: "Zip" Zabel, Chicago (NL), June 17, 1915
"Zip" was George Washington Zabel's nickname, and that's exactly how much energy he had left when he finished work on June 17, 1915. The Chicago Cubs reliever went 18⅓ innings for the 4–3 victory. He entered the game with two out in the first inning.

First pitcher to strike out 20 batters in nine innings

Roger Clemens, Boston, April 29, 1986
"Rocket" Roger Clemens of the Boston Red Sox rocketed past

Nolan Ryan, Tom Seaver and Steve Carlton in the baseball record books when he struck out 20 Seattle Mariners in a 3–1 win on April 29, 1986. Leftfielder Phil Bradley was Clemens's favorite victim—he was fanned four times. A decade later, on September 18, 1996, Clemens did it again. This time 20 Tigers were his victims in a 4–0 win in Detroit. Tiger Travis Fryman struck out four times.

Most strikeouts in a nine-inning National League game
20: Kerry Wood, Chicago, May 6, 1998
Don't mess with Texas! Lone Star State native Kerry Wood registered 20 strikeouts for the Chicago Cubs against the Houston Astros on May 6, 1998. Wood—who wore number 34 like Texan great Nolan Ryan—struck out the most players in a National League game and tied Roger Clemens, yet another Texan, for the major league record. But Wood and Clemens had company on May 8, 2001, when Randy Johnson fanned 20 for the Arizona Diamondbacks. Johnson, however, needed 11 innings to enter the 20 K club. And he's from California.

First pitcher to record four strikeouts in an inning in a World Series game
Orval Overall, Chicago (NL), October 14, 1908
The Detroit Tigers knew their World Series dreams were over when they met Orval Overall. The Chicago Cubs hurler began the fifth game of the 1908 World Series with four strikeouts on October 14. One of the batters got to first on a third-strike wild pitch. The Cubs won 2–0 to clinch the title with a three-hit shutout.

Only non-complete perfect game
Ernie Shore, Boston (AL), June 23, 1917
Babe Ruth was a "bad Bambino" in the eyes of umpire Brick

Owens one day in 1917. Owens tossed the Boston Red Sox starting pitcher from the game when he argued a walk given to the first Washington Senators batter he faced, Ray Morgan. Ernie Shore took to the mound in relief, and retired the next 26 batters to win 4–0 in the first game of a doubleheader.

First pitcher to throw a no-hitter in a clinching situation

Mike Scott, Houston, September 25, 1986

Mike Scott came up big when it mattered with an out-of-this-world performance for the Houston Astros against the San Francisco Giants on September 25, 1986. Scott clinched the 1986 National League West Division title with a 2–0, no-hit victory.

Earliest no-hitter in a season

Hideo Nomo, Boston, April 4, 2001

The back of his jersey said "Nomo," but Hideo Nomo's fans were calling him "No-no" after he debuted with the Boston Red Sox on April 4, 2001; the Japanese import had denied the Baltimore Orioles a hit in a Red Sox 3–0 win. It was the second no-hitter for Nomo, who no-hit the Colorado Rockies during a 9–0 Los Angeles Dodgers win in 1996.

Most consecutive major league no-hitters

2: Johnny Vander Meer, Cincinnati, 1938

Johnny Vander Meer was known as baseball's "Dutch Master" for a very good reason: his back-to-back no-hit masterpieces for the Cincinnati Reds were a major league first and only. Vander Meer didn't let any Boston Bees reach base safely on June 11, 1938, a 3–0 Reds home win. Then on June 15, Vander Meer stole the show in the first night game at Brooklyn's Ebbets Field by no-hitting the Dodgers 6–0.

Most no-hitters on the same day

2: *Ted Breitenstein, Cincinnati, and Jim Hughes, Baltimore, April 22, 1898*

2: *Dave Stewart, Oakland, and Fernando Valenzuela, Los Angeles, June 29, 1990*

For the second time in Ted Breitenstein's career, he came one batter shy of perfection when, as a Cincinnati Red, he walked one Pittsburgh Pirate and retired 27 in an 11–0 win. The first time was during his 1891 debut with the St. Louis Browns. The second time may have been twice as sweet, but he shared the spotlight with Jim Hughes of the Baltimore Orioles, who no-hit the Boston Beaneaters 8–0 on the same day. It took another 92 years for another no-hit "two-fer," when Dave Stewart of the Oakland Athletics blanked all Blue Jays batters 5–0 in Toronto—the same day that Fernando Valenzuela stifled the Cardinals in a Los Angeles Dodgers 6–0 victory.

Most walks allowed in a no-hitter

9: *A.J. Burnett, Florida, May 12, 2001*

Florida Marlins pitcher A.J. Burnett was in a giving mood in a 3–0 win over the San Diego Padres in 2001. He gave opposing batters everything but a hit. Of the nine walks allowed, Ryan Klesko and Bubba Trammell of the Padres had two apiece. Klesko, Rickey Henderson and Donaldo Mendez stole bases. Burnett topped the performance when he hit Padre batter Damian Jackson in the third inning.

Only pitcher to throw a no-hitter in his first start and never again pitch a complete game

"Bobo" Holloman, St. Louis (AL), May 6, 1953

You could call Alva Lee "Bobo" Holloman a one-game no-hit wonder. The St. Louis Browns pitcher no-hit the Philadelphia Athletics 6–0 in 1953. That was his first major league start. He played only 21 more games in his brief one-season major league career, and never pitched another complete game.

Most pitchers to combine for an extra-innings no-hitter
2: Francisco Cordova and Ricardo Rincon, Pittsburgh, July 12, 1997
The Houston Astros couldn't buy a hit the day they faced the "Veracruz connection" in 1997. Pittsburgh Pirates Francisco Cordova and Ricardo Rincon, both from the same Mexican city, joined forces to blank the Houston Astros 3–0. Cordova and Rincon also recorded the first extra-innings combined no-hitter. The game went into the 10th inning tied 0–0, when Mark Smith of the Pirates ended it with a three-run homer. Cordova pitched the first nine, giving up two walks and striking out 10. Rincon walked one and struck out one in relief.

Most no-hit losses to pitchers named Kevin
3: San Francisco Giants
Was it plain bad luck or a new ailment called "Kevinitis"? The San Francisco Giants suffered no-hit losses to pitchers named Kevin three times between 1992 and 2003. Kevin Gross gave the Los Angeles Dodgers a 2–0 no-hit performance on August 17, 1992; Kevin Brown led the charge in a 9–0 no-hitter on June 10, 1997, for the Florida Marlins, and Kevin Millwood of the Philadelphia Phillies completed the Kevin trilogy when he no-hit the Giants 1–0 on April 27, 2003.

Only one-hit/perfect game in major league history
Los Angeles vs. Chicago (NL), September 9, 1965
Baseball fans wanting hits were out of luck when the Los

Angeles Dodgers met the Chicago Cubs on September 9, 1965. They only saw one. Dodger ace Sandy Koufax registered a perfect 1–0 game while Cubs pitcher Bob Hendley yielded just one lonely hit to Dodger Lou Johnson, who scored the game's only run.

Most career one-hitters
12: Nolan Ryan and Bob Feller
Nolan Ryan could have had more than seven no-hitters. He pitched a record 12 one-hit games during his career. Bob Feller had a dozen, too, but he tossed just three no-hitters.

Tallest major league baseball players
Eric Hillman and Randy Johnson: six foot 10
If you were a batter facing pitchers Eric Hillman or Randy Johnson, you had to look up — way up. Hillman and Johnson were like towers on the pitching mound. Sure they could throw fast, but the first thing batters noticed was their height: six foot 10, to be exact. Hillman pitched for the New York Mets from 1992 to 1994. Johnson was at the height of his career when he shared the 2001 World Series' Most Valuable Player Award with fellow Arizona Diamondbacks pitcher Curt Schilling.

Busiest rookie pitcher
Irv Young, Boston (AL), 1905
Cy Young gets all the attention, but what about Irv? Irv who? Nicknamed "Cy the Second," the man from Maine pitched six major league years, racking up 378 innings — including 41 complete games — for the Boston Pilgrims in his 1905 rookie season. But Irv Young (no relation to Cy Young) never matched his 20–21 debut year and finished with a career 63–95 record. Cy Young still holds the career records for wins (511) and losses (315).

Most Cy Young Awards won

6: Roger Clemens

Some day they might rename the award for baseball's best pitcher the Roger Clemens Award. Clemens won six Cy Youngs, all in the American League, in 1986, 1987, 1991, 1997, 1998 and 2001.

Only pitcher to win the Cy Young Award in his final season

Sandy Koufax, Los Angeles, 1966

Arm pain cut short Sandy Koufax's Hall of Fame career, but at least it ended with some pleasure. The Los Angeles Dodgers southpaw was the National League's best pitcher in 1966, with a 27–9 record. The 30-year-old's performance was good enough to earn him his third unanimous Cy Young Award.

First pitcher to win Rookie of the Year and the Cy Young Award in the same season

Fernando Valenzuela, Los Angeles, 1981

After tequila and tacos, Fernando Valenzuela is Mexico's greatest export. The product of the Mexican League's Yucatan franchise was an instant hit with Los Angeles Dodgers fans when he ignited "Fernando mania" in the City of Angels. Valenzuela pitched 11 complete games and eight shutouts for a 13–7 record during the Dodgers' 1981 strike-shortened, World Series-winning season. After it was over, he was voted top rookie and top National League hurler. His new fans in America had plenty of reasons to say, *"Muchas gracias."*

First major leaguer to turn 100

Ralph Darwin Miller, March 15, 1973

Cincinnati-born pitcher Ralph Miller reached the century mark in innings pitched and hits allowed. He also hit the century mark in age. Miller saw action in just five National League games for Brooklyn and Baltimore in 1898 and 1899, but became the first ex-major leaguer to reach his 100th birthday. Miller died in Cincinnati on May 8, 1973—four days after the 75th anniversary of his first National League game.

First pitcher to record a shutout and hit a game-winning home run in the same game

Tom Hughes, Washington, August 3, 1906

The best offense is a good defense. And Tom Hughes of the Washington Senators provided just that against the St. Louis Browns in a 1906 game, when he scored its only run—the game-winning homer—in the 10th inning off St. Louis' Fred Glade. Never before had a pitcher won a game that ended with his own home run.

Most career home runs by a pitcher

38: Wes Ferrell

Opponents of the designated-hitter rule wish they could clone Wes Ferrell. He clubbed 38 home runs during his career: 37 as a pitcher and one as a pinch-hitter. In 1934, Ferrell even hit a pair of homers in two games for the Boston Red Sox: on July 13, 1934, in a 7–2 win over the St. Louis Browns, and on August 22, 1934, in a 3–2 win over the White Sox.

CHAPTER 3

Mound Madness

TALES FROM THE MOUND

It's called Mound Madness, and a few pitchers have been known to suffer from it. Think of Mark "The Bird" Fidrych, the Detroit Tigers pitcher who spoke to the ball in his glove before he sent it flying towards home plate. Fidrych brought childhood fun back to the game; he literally treated the mound as his own sandbox in the middle of a stadium. But every pitcher, good or bad, has a touch of mound madness—just like the Bird.

First pitcher to receive a university degree in a pre-game ceremony

Vern Ruhle, Detroit, August 6, 1975

Detroit Tigers rookie pitcher Vern Ruhle couldn't make it to his graduation ceremony at Michigan's Olivet College, so the ceremony came to him. President Dr. Ray Loeschner and Dean Dr. Donald Wilson presented Ruhle with his baccalaureate degree in business administration on-field while organist Dan Greet played "Pomp and Circumstance" and Olivet College's alma mater song. Unfortunately, the Baltimore Orioles spoiled the occasion by beating the Tigers 4–2. Ruhle did not see action.

Most famous ex-major league pitcher to work at a convenience store

Denny McLain

Slurpees, Big Gulps, Denny McLain. Denny McLain? What is he doing working at a 7-Eleven? In 2003, the ex-Detroit Tigers pitcher went to work as a clerk at the convenience store's Sterling Heights, Michigan, location as part of an eight-year federal prison sentence for embezzlement. McLain won 31 games in 1968—the first 30-plus-win season for a pitcher since Dizzy Dean accomplished it in 1934. But brushes with the law marred McLain's post-baseball life. In 1985, he was jailed for 23 years on convictions for drug dealing, loan sharking, bookmaking and extortion offences between 1978 and 1983. He was freed on appeal after three years served, but was later convicted of embezzlement, money laundering, mail fraud and conspiracy after $3 million went missing from his company's pension fund in 1997.

Most famous ticket-taker

Cy Young

The Boston Pilgrims needed relief at the gate of Huntington

Avenue Base Ball Grounds, so they called on Cy Young to take tickets. The pitching ace helped usher the overflow World Series Game 3 crowd of 18,801 into the ballpark on October 3, 1903, then pitched seven innings of relief in a losing cause. When Young returned to regular duty as pitcher, he beat the Pittsburgh Pirates 11–2 and 7–3 in the fifth and seventh games of the series. The Pilgrims eventually won the first postseason meeting with a National League champion, five games to three.

Only pitcher named after a 19th-century American president who was portrayed by a future president in a movie

Grover Cleveland Alexander

Hail to the pitching chief! Grover Cleveland Alexander was born during President Grover Cleveland's first term, in 1887, in Elba, Nebraska. One of 13 children, the future Hall of Famer recorded 28 rookie wins in 1911 for the Philadelphia Phillies. And although he battled epilepsy and alcoholism as an adult, he still managed 373 career victories. In 1952, future American president Ronald Reagan portrayed Alexander in the film *The Winning Team*.

First medical procedure named for a pitcher

Tommy John Surgery

Pity poor Frank Jobe, the doctor who saved Tommy John's career with a pioneering procedure. It's John's name, not Jobe's, that is forever attached to the now-common ligament transplant surgery. The southpaw tore a ligament in his left elbow while pitching for the Los Angeles Dodgers on July 17, 1974, and was facing retirement. So Jobe tried an experimental surgical technique on September 25, 1974, transfering a tendon from John's right arm to his left in a two-hour procedure at a hospital in Inglewood, California. John nursed his arm back to shape for the 1976 season, and remained in the game until 1985. Of his 288 wins in 26 seasons, more than half (164) came after Jobe wove his medical magic.

First pitcher to perform emergency cardiopulmonary resuscitation on an injured fan before a game

Doc Medich, Pittsburgh, April 11, 1976

If there wasn't a doctor in the house when the Pittsburgh Pirates came to town, there was always Doc Medich, the Bucs pitcher who was studying to be a medic at the University of Pittsburgh. Medich's pre-med training and his ability to perform under pressure came in particularly handy during a 1976 road trip to Philadelphia's Veterans Stadium when a spectator collapsed from a heart attack. Medich resuscitated the 73-year-old, who was later pronounced dead at Methodist Hospital. Later, while playing for the Texas Rangers, Medich gave first aid to a woman who suffered a heart attack at Baltimore's Memorial Stadium, July 17, 1978.

Biggest team-levied fine for a controversial autobiography

$100,000: David Wells, New York (AL)

Call him the "Bronx Big Mouth." New York Yankees pitcher David Wells was slapped with a $100,000 fine by his own team for the statements he made in his 2003 autobiography, *Perfect I'm Not! Boomer on Beer, Backaches and Baseball*. Yankees management believed the book sullied the century-old team's image. What was so controversial? Wells wrote that up to one-quarter of major leaguers use steroids. He also claimed to have been hung-over from binge drinking when he pitched a perfect game for the Yankees against the Minnesota Twins on May 17, 1998.

First pitcher transported to the mound
Don McMahon, Milwaukee, June 23, 1958
Why walk when you can ride in style? Milwaukee Braves reliever Don McMahon wouldn't have it any other way when he was shuttled from the bullpen at Milwaukee County Stadium in the sidecar of a motor scooter to relieve rookie starter Carl Willey, for a 7–0 win over the San Francisco Giants.

Most letters in surnames of pitching foes of record
25: VanLandingham vs. Christiansen, August 9, 1995
Their names would barely fit on their jerseys or the scoreboard, for when San Francisco Giants pitcher William VanLandingham beat Pittsburgh Pirate Jason Christiansen in a 1995 game, the pitchers had a total of 25 letters in their combined surnames. VanLandingham went eight innings and was the winning pitcher in the Giants' 4–3 decision. Christiansen got the loss.

First face-off between pitchers with palindrome surnames
Nen vs. Otto, August 3, 1994
The Florida Marlins sent Robb Nen to the mound the same day the Chicago Cubs' pitching roster included Dave Otto. Both hurlers have palindrome surnames, meaning the names are the same read backwards or forwards. Florida won 9–8 and Nen got his 13th save of the season on Rich Scheid's win. Otto was the second of four Cubs pitchers, but did not figure in the decision at Wrigley Field.

Only 20th-century meeting by pitchers with the same first and last names

Bobby Jones, Colorado, vs. Bobby Jones, New York (NL), *May 11, 1999*
Broadcasters resorted to using middle names when they described the pitchers in this game between the Colorado Rockies and New York Mets. The Denver-based Rockies used lefty Bobby (Mitchell) Jones to beat right-hander Bobby (Joseph) Jones of the Mets 8–5.

Best one-legged pitcher

Bert Shepard, Washington, 1945

On August 4, 1945, Bert Shepard made a relief appearance in the major leagues, and, in the process, gave people with disabilities hope. He allowed three hits in $5\frac{1}{3}$ innings for the Washington Senators in a 4–0 win over the Boston Red Sox—the opener of a doubleheader. Shepard lost his right leg below the knee when his fighter jet was shot down over France in May 1944.

Only 20th-century pitcher to throw "ambidextrously"

Greg Harris, Montreal, 1995
You've heard of a switch-hitter. How about a switch-pitcher? On September 28, 1995, Montreal Expos reliever Greg Harris pitched with both arms in the ninth inning. The Expos lost 9–7 to the Cincinnati Reds, but Harris didn't surrender a run. He faced two batters with his right arm and two with his left using a custom-made glove with six fingers. But Harris wasn't baseball's first pitcher to use both arms. Tony Mullane was the first, and he did it twice: July 18, 1882, and July 14, 1893. What set Mullane apart was the fact he lacked a key piece of equipment: he had no glove.

First minor league player fined for using tobacco

Travis Baptist, Knoxville (class AA), 1993

Pitcher Travis Baptist knows all about irony. He was slapped with a $100 fine for using smokeless tobacco on June 26, 1993, while playing in the class AA Southern League for the Knoxville Smokies. The fine was levied 11 days after cancer-causing snuff and chewing tobacco were banned from all minor league baseball circuits.

Pitcher with the most complex pre-pitch ritual

Ron Kline, 1952–1970

Ron Kline was a touchy-feely pitcher, who before every throw touched his cap, belt and shirt. Kline started for the first half of his 18-year career, then became a reliever who registered 108 saves. He led the National League with 18 losses in 1956, but led the American League in 1965 with 29 saves.

Only pitcher hit by a seagull's "fish bomb"

Ellis Kinder, St. Louis (AL), May 7, 1947

Something fishy happened to Ellis Kinder while he was pitching at Fenway Park in 1947, when the St. Louis Browns hurler became baseball's only victim of a fly-by fish bomb. But when a seagull dropped the three-pound smelt on Kinder, it didn't throw him off his game: he yielded six hits in a 4–2 win over the host Red Sox. Neither did it deter him from later playing in Fenway Park. He spent eight seasons of his 12–year career there.

First dove killed by a pitcher during a game

March 25, 2001

Randy Johnson is more than enough for a human batter to handle, but a dove? Well, let's just say the "Big Unit" won the duel. When a dove flew in front of a Johnson pitch — clocked at 95 miles per hour—during a spring training game on March 25, 2001, the only casualty was the bird. The Arizona Diamondbacks beat the San Francisco Giants 10–6.

First minor leaguer demoted for killing a bird

Jae-kuk Ryu, Florida Cubs (class AA)

If you want to get ahead in baseball's minor leagues, refrain from killing an osprey. Jae-kuk Ryu didn't, and earned a demotion from the class A Florida Cubs in Daytona Beach to the Lansing Lugnuts of Michigan in the Midwest League. The South Korean-born hurler hit Ozzy the Osprey in his nest atop a 40-foot pole near left field before a game on April 21, 2003. Ozzy died six days later at the Audubon Birds of Prey Center in Maitland, Florida. To make amends, Ryu's ex-team auctioned balls autographed by Chicago Cubs players and sent the proceeds, along with $1 from every ticket sold for their April 25 game, to a local animal clinic.

Most unbelievable injury explanation

Eric Show, 1992

Eric Show was not fit to even pick up a ball when he reported for spring training with the Oakland Athletics in 1992. Both of his hands were bandaged. The pitcher claimed he had cut them climbing a barbed wire fence as he fled from attackers at a convenience store. The A's sent him home, and he never played again. Show, who was released from the San Diego Padres the previous fall, was a Renaissance man who turned to drugs and alcohol to battle his inner demons. The former University of California Riverside physics major played jazz guitar and espoused far right-wing politics. Over 11 years in the majors, he won 101 games, but was best remembered for allowing Pete Rose's record-breaking 4,192nd career hit in 1985. That dubious honor sent him into a depression. Show was only 37 when he died from a heroin and cocaine overdose on March 16, 1994.

Only pitcher injured by a watermelon
Jay Witasick, San Diego, 2003

Jay Witasick knows how to pitch, but he found out the hard way that he needs coaching on his watermelon disposal technique. The San Diego Padres right-hander strained his throwing arm during spring training in March 2003, but not on the field. He suffered the injury throwing out trash containing watermelon. He later admitted to manager Bruce Bochy that he should have used his left arm instead. In the off-season, Witasick had signed a two-year deal with the team for $2.75 million.

Most teams in a career
12: Deacon McGuire, 1884–1912
12: Mike Morgan, 1978–2002

Deacon McGuire and Mike Morgan played for a dozen teams each, collecting more jerseys than any other players in major league history—or any professional sport, for that matter. Catcher McGuire played 26 seasons for the American Association's Toledo Blue Stockings, Cleveland Spiders, Rochester and Washington Senators; the National League's Detroit Wolverines, Philadelphia Phillies, Washington Senators and Brooklyn Dodgers, and the American League's Detroit Tigers, New York Yankees, Boston Red Sox and Cleveland Indians. Mike Morgan debuted in 1978 out of high school with the Oakland Athletics. His tour around the big leagues included stints with the New York Yankees, Toronto Blue Jays, Seattle Mariners, Baltimore Orioles, Los Angeles Dodgers,

Chicago Cubs, St. Louis Cardinals, Cincinnati Reds, Minnesota Twins, Texas Rangers and Arizona Diamondbacks. He finally won a World Series with Arizona in 2001.

Most teams beaten by a pitcher, career

30: Al Leiter

No team was immune from the wrath of Al Leiter. When Leiter registered a 10–1 win for the New York Mets over the Arizona Diamondbacks on April 30, 2002, he became the first major league pitcher to beat all 30 franchises.

Most team switches

16: Bobo Newsom, 1929–1953

If they ever make a movie about Bobo Newsom, the title should be *Here Today, Gone Tomorrow, Be Back Soon*. Newsom's 20 big-league years included five stints with the Washington Senators, three with the St. Louis Browns and two each with the Philadelphia Athletics and Brooklyn Dodgers. (Maybe it was the taste of bigger things to come: all of those teams later relocated.) Newsom was also a Chicago Cub, Detroit Tiger and New York Yankee. The three-time, 20-game loser also won 20 twice. He was 21–5 in 1940 with the Tigers, pitching three complete games in the World Series. Unfortunately for Newsom, he lost Game 7 by a score of 2–1 to the Cincinnati Reds.

Biggest fine for a player watching his own team play outside an opponent's ballpark

$500: Tom Browning, Cincinnati, July 7, 1993

Tom Browning owed his Cincinnati Reds manager Davey Johnson plenty of greenbacks and an explanation after he left Wrigley Field to watch his team win from across the street. Browning wanted a glimpse of Wrigleyville's legendary atmosphere, so he put a sweatshirt over his jersey and went to the roof of a three-storey building on Sheffield Avenue to watch the Reds win 4–3. Browning was slapped with a $500 fine, likely the most anyone ever paid to watch the Reds play at Wrigley from beyond the so-called "Friendly Confines."

Biggest fine for breaking a camera during a game

$15,000: Curt Schilling, Arizona

Curt Schilling doesn't like being on Major League Baseball's "candid camera." So he didn't mind paying a $15,000 fine when he deliberately broke one during a 5–1 loss to the visiting San Diego Padres on May 24, 2003. It wasn't any old camera, either. It was the QuesTec Umpire Evaluation System camera, which monitors every ball and strike called by an umpire. Schilling is not alone in his opposition to the camera, however. The World Umpires Association claims QuesTec is inaccurate and inconsistent.

Pitcher with the worst non-illicit habit

Sparky Lyle

The word among big leaguers was: Never leave veteran relief pitcher Sparky Lyle alone with a birthday cake. Lyle, who played from 1967 to 1982, often made birthday celebrants the butt of his practical jokes—literally—when he would sit, bare-bottomed, on a birthday boy's cake (before the candles were placed and lit, of course). Lyle notched 238 saves and a 99–38 record before reaching the end of his 16-year career. (If you're a victim seeking revenge, mark July 22 on your calendar. That's Lyle's birthday.)

Most boxes of Jell-O demanded in a contract

37: Charlie Kerfeld, Houston

Charlie Kerfeld had a career year in 1986, but champagne wouldn't do to celebrate. Instead, he chose Jell-O. The Houston Astros pitcher won 11 games and saved seven when Houston won the

National League's West Division title, so he wanted a raise. Since teammate Jim Deshaies got $100,000, Kerfeld asked for $110,037.37, plus 37 boxes of Jell-O. Kerfeld loved to eat the gelatin and pudding snacks, but 37 boxes? That was his jersey number.

Most expensive shirt

$250: Johnny Allen, Cleveland

Umpire Bill McGowan must have felt like Johnny Allen's mother on June 7, 1938, when he told the Cleveland Indians pitcher to change his shirt or leave the game. (Although the offending clothing was worn under his Indians jersey, the tattered sleeves were exposed.) An angry Allen went to the clubhouse and never returned, so manager Oscar Vitt fined him $250 for going AWOL. Indians owner Alva Bradley later bought the infamous shirt for $250 to display at a Cleveland department store owned by his brother.

Only pitcher to admit throwing a no-hitter while under the influence of a psychedelic drug

Dock Ellis, Pittsburgh, June 12, 1970

Dock Ellis wouldn't share a hit with the host San Diego Padres — in more ways than one. Ellis tossed a 2–0 no-hitter for the Pittsburgh Pirates on June 12, 1970, then claimed to have done so while "tripping" on lysergic acid diethylamide, better known as LSD.

Only pitcher to be hit by lightning and finish a game

Ray Caldwell, Cleveland, August 8, 1919

Thunder and lightning were no big deal to Cleveland Indians pitcher Ray Caldwell. The spitballer was one out away from beating the Philadelphia Athletics when he got a jolt from a bolt and fell to the ground. But the hair-raising experience didn't prevent him from getting back on the mound to retire the next batter and register a 2–1 win.

CHAPTER 4

On Target

CATCHING CRAZINESS

Yogi Berra, one of the game's greatest catchers, once said: "Baseball is 90 per cent mental. The other half is physical." And although Berra's math may be fuzzy, the sentiment is true. If you're a catcher, you must be an oddball to offer your padded hand as a target for a hard white ball that travels a 60-foot-six-inch flight path in the blink of an eye.

Last catcher without a helmet

Bob Montgomery, Boston, 1979

Boston Red Sox catcher Bob Montgomery, the last ballplayer without a "hard hat," finished his career with a reinforced fielding cap instead of a helmet. Montgomery debuted in 1970 and was a catcher for 10 seasons.

Most catchers on a team to suffer broken hands in the same inning

2: Tim McCarver and Mike Ryan, Philadelphia, 1970

Being a Philadelphia Phillies catcher was an occupational hazard on May 2, 1970. The Phillies were visiting San Francisco for a game with the Giants, when Tim McCarver broke a bone in his hand on a foul tip in the sixth inning. He was replaced behind the plate by Mike Ryan. Next, Willie Mays singled and Willie McCovey had an RBI double. When Ken Henderson singled to right field and McCovey was thrown out at home plate, McCovey spiked Ryan's hand. Ryan left the game with a broken hand and was replaced by Jim Hutto. The Giants were 7–1 winners, but at least Hutto finished the game with two healthy hands.

Most languages spoken by a catcher

12: Moe Berg

Lefty Gomez said of Moe Berg: "He speaks a dozen languages and can't hit in any of them." And he was right. Berg had a career .243 batting average and hit only six home runs in 15 years, but he did speak English, French, Spanish, German, Italian, Greek, Hebrew, Hungarian, Russian, Japanese, Sanskrit and Gaelic. Of course, Russian and Hebrew were obvious accomplishments, because Berg was born in New York City to a Russian-Jewish immigrant family, March 2, 1902. But Berg was also among the best-schooled major leaguers. He attended Ivy

League universities Princeton and Columbia in the U.S.A., as well as the Sorbonne in Paris, France.

Most seasons catching

26: Deacon McGuire, 1884–1912

Baseball's most durable catcher was also its most mobile. Deacon McGuire caught for a record 26 seasons, mostly in the 19th century, and switched teams 10 times. He debuted in 1884 with the American Association's Toledo Blue Stockings, played with the National League's Detroit Wolverines and Philadelphia Phillies, then returned to the American Association to play for the Cleveland Spiders, Rochester Hop Bitters and Washington Senators. And when the Senators moved to the National League in 1892, McGuire moved with them. He also saw action with the Brooklyn Superbas, Detroit Tigers, New York Yankees, Boston Red Sox and Cleveland Naps before retiring in 1912 with the Tigers. McGuire's last game was a contest between Detroit and Philadelphia, in which Detroit fielded a team of amateurs after the real Tigers went on strike to protest Ty Cobb's suspension. The 48-year-old McGuire singled in two at-bats.

Most innings caught in one day

28: Ossee Schreckengost, Philadelphia (AL), July 4, 1905

For most Americans, the Fourth of July is a welcome summer day off to spend with friends and family. But not for Philadelphia Athletics catcher Ossee Schreckengost, who made history with a 28-inning performance in a 1905 day-night doubleheader. The Athletics swept the twinbill 5–2 and 4–2. The second game featured a 20-inning duel between Athletic Rube Waddell and Boston's Cy Young. And Schreckengost always showed his best whenever Waddell was on the mound. (Hint: The two were roommates on the road, and Waddell's contract barred him from eating crackers in bed. Schreckengost simply couldn't tolerate the crumbs or sleep through the loud munching.)

Most no-hitters caught
4: Ray Schalk, Chicago (AL)
There are two sides to every no-hitter story. Chicago White Sox catcher Ray Schalk had four such epics to his credit—including catching a perfect game by Charles Robertson on April 30, 1922, when Robertson beat the Detroit Tigers 2–0. Schalk's most productive year for "no-nos" was 1914, when he caught two during the month of May.

Most consecutive games with a hit by a rookie catcher
34: Benito Santiago, San Diego, 1987
Benito Santiago is to catching what Joe DiMaggio is to hitting. The San Diego Padre rookie reached base safely in 34 consecutive games during 1987. But his streak ended October 3 against Orel Hershiser when he went 0-for-3 in a 1–0 San Diego win over the Dodgers. Santiago's play earned him National League Rookie of the Year honors. The streak was the longest ever by a catcher.

Most home runs by a catcher
351: Carlton Fisk, 1969–1993
He could catch the ball and he knew how to hit it a long way, too. In fact, Carlton Fisk cracked 351 home runs as a Boston Red Sox and Chicago White Sox catcher. But his most famous homer was in Game 6 of the 1975 World Series, a 12th-inning blast that gave the Red Sox a 7–6 win over the Cincinnati Reds (who eventually won in seven games).

Biggest fine for a bullpen catcher caught possessing marijuana

$5,000: Carlos Luis Perez, Montreal

There was weed in the Montreal Expos bullpen, even though the Olympic Stadium is carpeted with AstroTurf. Expos bullpen catcher Carlos Luis Perez pleaded guilty to possessing half a kilogram of marijuana with intent to export when he was busted at Montreal's ballpark on September 27, 2002. The judge levied a $5,000 fine.

Only known spy in major league baseball

Moe Berg

You've heard of *Catcher in the Rye*, but did you know about the catcher who was a spy, Moe Berg? After his baseball career, Berg worked full-time with the Central Intelligence Agency's predecessor, the Office of Strategic Services, spying on the Nazis' atomic bomb project during World War II. There is evidence that he was also a part-time spy during his catching career. When the American League All-Stars barnstormed Japan in 1934, for example, Berg took time out to do reconnaissance work for the American government. His photographs were later used to prepare for the bombing of Tokyo in World War II.

Most famous home-plate collision

Pete Rose and Ray Fosse, July 14, 1970

Cleveland Indians catcher Ray Fosse found out the hard way that Cincinnati Red Pete Rose was unstoppable, when, in the 12th inning of the 1970 All-Star game, Rose broke a 4–4 tie but also broke Fosse's shoulder. Before a hometown crowd at Cincinnati's Riverfront Stadium, Rose gave the National League the 5–4 win when he collided with Fosse at home plate on Jim Hickman's single. Rose's aggressiveness was uncharacteristic of an All-Star game, but not for baseball's future all-time hit king, who was nick-named "Charlie Hustle" for his hard-nosed, competitive style of play. Fosse's season would later end with a broken index finger.

Only catcher for both Ted Williams and Babe Ruth
Joe Glenn

Joe Glenn is one of the most envied men in America: he got paid to play catch at Yankee Stadium with the "Bambino" and at Fenway Park with the "Splendid Splinter." Glenn was the other half of the New York Yankees battery on May 1, 1933, when Babe Ruth pitched a complete game—a 6–5 victory over the visiting Boston Red Sox. Glenn later played for the Red Sox and was behind the plate when Ted Williams made his only appearance on the mound during two innings of a 12–1 loss to the Detroit Tigers at Fenway Park, August 24, 1940.

First player to catch a ball dropped from the Washington Monument
William "Pop" Schriver, August 25, 1884

"Pop" Schriver made a monumental catch in 1884. The Chicago White Stockings catcher stood 555 feet below the Washington Monument in the nation's capital while pitcher Clark Griffith threw the ball from the observation deck.

First catcher to wear glasses
Clint Courtney, St. Louis (AL), 1952

St. Louis Browns catcher Clint Courtney had 20/20 vision behind the plate, thanks to his eyeglasses, which he wore under his mask without fear they'd be broken by a foul tip. Courtney caught 119 games for the Browns in 1952, and played another 11 seasons.

Most SuperBalls found exiting a bat by a catcher

6: Bill Freehan, Detroit, September 7, 1974

Graig Nettles had too much bounce when he wished he had a blast. The New York Yankees batter broke his bat while hitting a single in 1974 against the Detroit Tigers—after earlier hitting a home run with the same stick. Tigers catcher Bill Freehan subsequently found six rubber SuperBalls spilling out of Nettles's broken bat as it lay on-field. Nettles was called out on the single, but his earlier homer stood as the winner in the 1–0 game. Nettles's explanation for the SuperBalls was less than super. A fan in Chicago, he claimed, gave him the bat for good luck.

Only catcher to pitch twice in the same season

Rick Cerone, New York (AL), 1987

Rick Cerone was an expert at catchin' and throwin'. In fact, twice in 1987, the New York Yankees catcher saw action behind the plate and on the mound. On July 19, Cerone pitched the last inning of a 20–3 loss to the Texas Rangers in Arlington, entering the game with the bases loaded and none out and pitching to backup catcher Mark Salas. Two runners scored—one on a ground ball and the other on a balk. Cerone struck out one Ranger after one inning, but wasn't charged with the runs. Then on August 9, Cerone pitched a scoreless eighth inning in a 15–4 loss to Detroit and allowed just one walk.

First catcher traded for himself

Harry Chiti, 1962

Catcher Harry Chiti was never involved in a blockbuster trade, but he was a special commodity in one transaction. During 1961's off-season, Chiti was traded like a hot potato, going from the Detroit Tigers to Baltimore Orioles on October 11 and then to the Cleveland Indians on November 16. But he never appeared in a game for the Tribe, who sent him to the New York Mets on April

26, 1962, for a player to be named later. On June 15, Chiti was revealed as that player when the Mets shipped him back to Cleveland after only 15 games.

Most famous catchers brawl

Thurman Munson vs. Carlton Fisk, August 1, 1973

It was a battle of epic proportions. Thurman Munson of the New York Yankees and Cartlon Fisk of the Boston Red Sox went toe-to-toe in a 1973 game at Fenway Park, with the score tied 2–2 in the top of the ninth. Munson led off the Yankees' ninth with a double, moved to third on a Graig Nettles missed bunt and was caught stealing in a collision at home with Fisk. The players clashed as they tried to regain their footing and were subsequently ejected. Bob Montgomery took Fisk's spot and scored the game-winning run.

Most confusing battery

Mark Redman and Mike Redmond, Florida, 2003

At least they didn't play for the Reds or Red Sox. Fans, players and play-by-play announcers alike were equally confused when the Florida Marlins paired pitcher Mark Redman and catcher Mike Redmond in 2003. On April 29 of that year, Redmond pinch-hit for Redman in a 7–5 Florida win at Arizona. And when he threw a career-high 11 strikeouts in a complete-game four-hitter 9–4 win over Milwaukee on April 24, 2003, Redman's performance was mistakenly credited to Redmond. Redman also got his first major league hit with a bat that was intended for delivery to Redmond. Although they were both nicknamed "Red," the men were easily distinguished on the field: five-foot-11, 210-pound Seattle-native Redmond wore 52; San Diego-born, six-foot-five, 245-pound Redman had number 55.

CHAPTER 5

History Sticks

BATTING BRILLIANCE

AND BANALITY

Once they were tall trees standing in forests, ignoring the laws of gravity as they grew skyward. When the time came, they were chopped down and made into bats. Some were polished and treated like the best of friends, others were broken and discarded. But these wooden wonders were always there when some of the game's great and not-so-great offensive feats were performed.

Longest hitting streak in professional baseball

61 games: Joe DiMaggio, San Francisco (PCL), 1933

Nice try Joe, but you're just not as good as you were in the minors. (Well, at least in the realm of hitting in consecutive games.) For in 1941, when Joe DiMaggio set a major league record with hits in 56 straight games for the New York Yankees, he fell short of his personal best. DiMaggio was just 18 years old when he hit safely in 61 games in a row during the 1933 San Francisco Seals' Pacific Coast League season. That streak ended July 26, 1933, when pitcher Ed Walsh Jr. of the Oakland Oaks stopped him.

First player to hit for the cycle in both leagues

Bob Watson, Houston and Boston

Bob who? Watson, my dear. Of all the players who saw action in the majors, it was Bob Watson who was first to hit for the cycle in both the National and American Leagues. Watson singled, doubled, tripled and homered for the Houston Astros in a 6–5 win against the San Francisco Giants on June 24, 1977. He did it again on September 15, 1979, for the Boston Red Sox, who beat the Baltimore Orioles 10–2.

Only 20-20-20 hitter nicknamed after a play and a racehorse

Frank "Wildfire" Schulte, Chicago (NL)

"Wildfire" Schulte was raging in 1911, the year the Chicago Cubs outfielder became the first to hit more than 20 doubles, triples and home runs (30, 21 and 21). The feat earned him the National League's Most Valuable Player honors and the Chalmers automobile prize, but the nickname came later. Schulte was a fan of actress Lillian Russell, so he named one of his thoroughbred racehorses after her play, *Wildfire*. Schulte's teammates and Chicago reporters eventually began calling the Cubs hitting and fielding star, "Wildfire."

Most batting triple crowns

2: Rogers Hornsby and Ted Williams

Who are the kings of baseball? Rogers Hornsby and Ted Williams acquitted themselves with royal valor on the diamond twice. Hornsby won the triple crown in 1922 and 1925 for the St. Louis Cardinals, with 152 RBIs, 42 home runs and a .401 average. And he did it again in 1925, with 39 home runs, 143 RBIs and a .403 average. Williams was a double triple winner in 1942 and 1947.

First batting average champion to wear eyeglasses

Chick Hafey, St. Louis (NL), 1931

Chick Hafey had eyes for a well-pitched ball in 1931, thanks to the glasses he wore. He hit .349 for the St. Louis Cardinals that year, eclipsing New York Giant Bill Terry and St. Louis Cardinal Jim Bottomley in baseball's closest three-man race for the title. Hafey would later retire with a .317 lifetime average, but could have been a bigger star without the vision and sinus problems that marred his career since the day he was hit with two pitches in a 1926 game. When he left after only 15 games in the 1935 season, Commissioner Kenesaw Mountain Landis waived the $1,500 fine and put Hafey on the voluntary disabled list.

Most bases in a game

19: Shawn Green, Los Angeles, May 23, 2002

Los Angeles Dodgers rightfielder Shawn Green was batting clean-up in Milwaukee, but made quite a mess for the host Brewers when he saw more bases than balls, racking up 19 total bases in the 2003 game at Miller Field. Green had six hits, six runs and seven RBIs in the 16–3 Dodgers win. Four of his hits were home runs.

Most RBIs in an inning by a player

8: Fernando Tatis, St. Louis, April 23, 1999

It was the most productive inning of Fernando Tatis's career and the worst of Chan Ho Park's. Tatis came to the plate twice for the St. Louis Cardinals in the third inning of a 1999 game against Park and the Los Angeles Dodgers, hitting grand slams both times. The Cardinals turned Tatis's outburst into a 12–5 win.

Most RBIs in a game

12: Jim Bottomley, St. Louis (NL), September 16, 1924
12: Mark Whiten, St. Louis, September 7, 1993

Are they the St. Louis Cardinals or the St. Louis CaRBInals? The Redbirds boast the only players to record a dozen RBIs in a game. "Sunny" Jim Bottomley collected his dozen when his team beat the host Brooklyn Robins 17–3 in a 1924 game. Bottomley had a trio of singles, a double and a pair of home runs—one of which was a grand slam. Sixty-nine years later, Mark Whiten smacked a grand slam, a pair of three-run homers and a two-run shot in a 15–2 Cardinals win over the Cincinnati Reds.

Most RBIs in a game by a player who drove in all his team's runs

Mike Greenwell, Boston, September 2, 1996

Boston Red Sox Mike Greenwell was a one-man traveling band against the Seattle Mariners in 1996—all the offense his team needed in a 10-inning, 9–8 road win. He singled and doubled and smacked two home runs—one of them a seventh-inning grand slam—to finish the day 4-for-5 at the plate with all nine RBIs.

Worst performance at the plate

0-for-11: Tony Boeckel and Charlie Pick, Boston (NL), May 1, 1920

If at first you don't succeed, try and try again. But if you can't get a hit after 11 trips to the plate, you really don't deserve a 12th try. And that's just what happened to Boston Braves Tony Boeckel and Charlie Pick, who both went 0-for-11 at the plate against the Brooklyn Robins during a marathon 1–1 tie game on May 1, 1920.

Best slump-killer
Morganna Roberts, August 31, 1969

Morganna Roberts is magic, according to Atlanta Brave Clete Boyer. The ample-chested exotic dancer, known as baseball's "kissing bandit," sprang Boyer from a 1-for-17 batting slump in 1969. During a game against the Chicago Cubs, Roberts ambushed Boyer in the on-deck circle when nobody was looking, then planted a smooch on his lips when everybody was looking. Boyer immediately ripped an RBI single. Despite his team's 8–4 loss, he finished the day 3-for-4. Boyer reached base eight times during his next 15 at-bats.

Smallest batter
Three foot seven: Eddie Gaedel, St. Louis (AL), 1951
St. Louis Browns owner Bill Veeck gave the American League a small gift for its 75th anniversary. How small? Three foot seven— that's what Eddie Gaedel measured. The smallest batter in major league history faced Detroit Tigers pitcher Bob Cain in the only trip to the plate of his career on August 19, 1951, the day Veeck celebrated the AL's birthday. Gaedel, wearing jersey number ⅛, walked, but was immediately replaced by pinch-runner Jim Delsing. The Tigers won the second game of the doubleheader 6–2. As for Veeck, the AL was not amused. It barred Gaedel and other midgets from playing baseball.

Biggest batting average decrease for a batting champion

118 points: Norm Cash, Detroit, 1962

Norm Cash went from being 1961 batting champ to 1962 batting chump. He was .361 in 1961, when he homered 41 times and had 132 RBIS. But although he managed 39 homers in 1962, his average fell 118 points to .243. Cash came clean when he later admitted to doctoring his bat in 1961 with a mixture of sawdust, cork and glue through a hole drilled in the barrel. Cash would play 17 seasons, including 15 in a Tigers uniform, and never again hit .300.

Most batting average championships

12: Ty Cobb, 1907–1919

Ty Cobb led the American League in batting averages 12 times over 13 seasons between 1907 and 1919. But his best year was 1911, when he hit .420. Cleveland Indian Tris Speaker broke Cobb's streak in 1916 by batting .386 — .15 points better than Cobb.

Highest career batting average

1.000: Chuck Lindstrom, Chicago (AL), and John Paciorek, Houston

Easy come, easy go. Chuck Lindstrom caught one game for the Chicago White Sox on September 28, 1958, collecting an RBI triple, a walk and a run to finish his career with a perfect batting average. His White Sox beat the Kansas City Athletics 11–4. John Paciorek, too, was never seen again in the big leagues despite a dazzling debut on September 29, 1963. He walked twice and was 3-for-3, with three RBIs and four runs.

First trade of a defending home-run champion for a defending batting champion

Rocky Colavito for Harvey Kuenn, April 17, 1960

In 1960, the Detroit Tigers wanted a slugger and the Cleveland Indians wanted better hitting. So Detroit sent Harvey Kuenn — who in 1959 led the American League with a .353 batting average — to the Indians for Rocky Colavito. (In 1959, Colavito's 42 home runs shared top spot with Harmon Killebrew's.) But the trade turned out to be a bust. Neither the players, nor their teams, equaled their 1959 performances.

First designated hitter

Ron Blomberg, New York (AL), April 6, 1973

New York Yankee Ron Blomberg liked to joke about his small place in baseball history, sometimes calling himself the "designated Jew." But he was the majors' first designated hitter on Opening Day 1973, when he drew a walk from Boston Red Sox pitcher Luis Tiant in his first at-bat. In this game, the new rule didn't matter. Blomberg was 1-for-3 and the Yankees lost to the Red Sox 15–5.

First designated hitter to play a full season

Rusty Staub, Detroit, 1978

Rusty Staub got to do something in 1978 with the Detroit Tigers that he never got to try during his years with the Houston Astros, Montreal Expos and New York Mets — bat every game for an entire season without fielding. Staub played all 162 games as the Tigers' designated hitter. His .273 average was far from a career best, but he did drive in 121 runs. (Staub played all 162 games in 1971 for the Expos, but that was in his capacity as an outfielder.)

First National League designated hitter in an interleague game

Glenallen Hill, San Francisco, June 12, 1997

Baseball purists who detest the designated-hitter rule bemoan the day Glenallen Hill became the first National League regular-season DH. The Giants were in Arlington, Texas, in 1997, to face the Rangers in baseball's first interleague game. American League rules prevailed, so the Giants used a DH. Hill was 0-for-3 with one RBI in the 4–3 Giants win.

Longest wait for a free watch

41 years: Carvel "Bama" Rowell, Boston (NL)

Watches measure time in seconds, minutes and hours, but Boston Brave "Bama" Rowell would count 41 years from when he won a Bulova to when he collected his prize. Rowell hit the Bulova clock atop the scoreboard in Boston on May 30, 1946, during a 10–8 win over the Brooklyn Dodgers in the second half of a doubleheader. But it wasn't until 1987 that Rowell got his watch. There was only one thing he could say: "It's about time!"

Last pitcher to bat .300+ and win 20+ games in a season

Jim "Catfish" Hunter, Oakland, 1971

Oakland Athletics pitcher "Catfish" Hunter was .350 at the plate and 21–11 on the mound in 1971, making him an all-round offensive and defensive threat in his seventh of 15 major league seasons.

Most pitchers faced by a batter in an American League inning

3: Ted Williams, Boston (AL), July 4, 1948

The Philadelphia Athletics couldn't remove the "Splendid Splinter" when they sent three different pitchers to the mound against Ted Williams on the Fourth of July in 1948. Boston broke a 5–5 tie to beat the A's 20–8 at Fenway Park on the power of 14 runs and 14 RBIs in one inning. Williams and Bobby Doerr drew a record-tying two walks each.

Best batting improvement after a haircut
Vladimir Guerrero, Montreal, April 19, 2003

Unlike the legendary Samson, Montreal Expo Vladimir Guerrero gained power with less hair when a teammate helped him cut short a slump. On April 19, 2003, Guerrero came to play the Cincinnati Reds—a day-night double-header in San Juan, Puerto Rico—with an Afro, but left with shaved sides and a trim. Henry Mateo's scissor magic between games put an end to a 4-for-24 slump and helped Guerrero go 3-for-3 with a home run and five RBIs. The Expos swept the Reds 8–7 and 9–5.

Most unusual prize for hitting a flagpole
Fertilizer

The Cincinnati Reds were having difficulty growing hits and runs on April 22, 1915, but it was Bill Hinchman of the Pittsburgh Pirates who won a container of fertilizer. In the bottom of the seventh, the Pirates rightfielder hit a ball off the flagpole for an inside-the-park homer, an unintended feat of accuracy that earned Hinchman 25 pounds of Radium fertilizer. He shared the 8–2 victory with his teammates.

Only batter killed in a major league game
Ray Chapman, Cleveland, August 17, 1920

On August 17, 1920, the Cleveland Indians' star shortstop Ray Chapman was hit on the head by an underhanded pitch from

New York Yankee Carl Mays. Chapman fell to the ground, was helped up by teammates and tried walking to the center-field clubhouse. At second base, however, he collapsed again and never regained consciousness. He died 12 hours later at a New York City hospital of complications from a broken skull. Chapman was deeply mourned by his teammates, who wore black armbands and dedicated their first World Series victory in his honor. (The Indians beat the Brooklyn Robins in seven games, and Chapman's widow received his $3,986.34 winner's share.) Cleveland fans so adored Chapman that 6,000 rosebuds were distributed in his memory at Municipal Stadium on the first anniversary of his death in 1921. As for Mays, he went 27–9 in 1921 and retired after a 15-year career in 1929.

Best strikeout to at-bat ratio

One strikeout per 62.6 at-bats: Joe Sewell
During 7,182 at-bats in 1,903 games over 14 years, Joe Sewell fanned just 114 times. In 1925, he had a career-best 608 at-bats and just four strikeouts. Things could have been different had he met Arlas Taylor more than once. On September 15, 1921, the Philadelphia Athletics pitcher registered just one career strikeout during two innings pitched—giving him a one-game, two-inning career on the mound. His lone victim was Sewell, who struck out just once for every 62.6 at-bats in his career. The Indians were 17–3 winners.

Most no-hit bids ruined

5: Cesar Tovar and Eddie Milner
They're the party-pooping, no-hitter wrecking crew. Pitchers hoping for a no-hitter didn't like it when Cesar Tovar or Eddie Milner came to the plate. The two players are tied for breaking up the most no-hit bids in big league history.

Most consecutive foul balls hit on Opening Day

15: *Luke Appling, Chicago, April 16, 1940*

Opposing pitchers never wanted to see Luke Appling in a foul mood. During a 1940 game against the New York Yankees, the Chicago White Sox shortstop fouled off 24 of Red Ruffing's pitches and then walked! (Appling claimed after the White Sox 8–2 win that his fouls were intentional.) But Appling met his match earlier in the year, on April 16, 1940, when he fouled 15 of Bob Feller's pitches consecutively. It did little to ruffle the Cleveland Indians pitcher, who registered the only Opening Day no-hitter with a 1–0 win.

Most consecutive-hit batters from the start of a game

3: *Pete Rose, Joe Morgan, Dan Driessen, Cincinnati, May 1, 1974*

Pittsburgh Pirates pitcher Dock Ellis wasn't striking out his batters in a 1974 start, he was striking them. Ellis intentionally hit Pete Rose, Joe Morgan and Dan Driessen to begin a game against the Cincinnati Reds on May 1, then walked Tony Perez, the Reds' fourth batter, before being yanked in the first inning of his team's 5–3 loss.

Most intentional walks in a career without a hit

1: *Neil Wilson, San Francisco, and Rex Johnston, Pittsburgh*

Imagine the thrill of playing in the major leagues and coming to bat. Then imagine the disappointment when you don't even get a chance to swing. That's what happened to catcher Neil Wilson of the 1960 Giants and outfielder Rex Johnston of the 1964 Pirates, who were both intentionally walked. Wilson had 10 at-bats and struck out twice, but was tabbed with one free pass that season. Johnston was walked three times, but never hit the ball.

Most money offered by suffragettes per run

$5: *May 18, 1915*

More than 4,100 women campaigning for the right to vote bought tickets to see the Chicago Cubs play the Giants at New York's Polo Grounds on May 18, 1915. They were also campaigning for runs by offering a $5 incentive to every player who scored on Suffrage Day. Only Chicago's Frank "Wildfire" Schulte left $5 richer, thanks to the first-inning run he scored. The visitors were 1–0 winners.

Only ex-bat boy with a number one rap single

Stanley Burrell

He didn't get a hit in the major leagues, but he did get a hit on the pop charts. Oakland Athletics bat boy Stanley Burrell was nick-named "Little Hammer" by A's players because he looked like "Hammerin'" Hank Aaron. Even team owner Charlie Finley had a soft spot for the charismatic teenager. He made him an honorary vice-president. Burrell went on to use MC Hammer as his stage name, and sold more than 10 million albums in 1990 on the strength of the hit single, "You Can't Touch This."

Most singles in a season without holding a bat

2: Napoleon Lajoie, Cleveland, 1906

"Look ma, no hands!" Nap Lajoie led the American League in 1906 with 214 hits for the Cleveland Indians, including a pair in which he connected with the ball after letting go of his bat.

CHAPTER 6

Round-Trippers

THERE'S NO PLACE

LIKE HOME

Everybody wants to be the hero, the batter who hits the ball and touches them all. It's not as easy as it looks, but it's the simplest way to travel across three bags to reach home. Throughout baseball history, some players have made slugging their art. Others have done the job ugly.

Only home run allowed off a head

Jose Canseco, Texas, May 26, 1993

Texas Ranger Jose Canseco was always told to use his head to play baseball, though never like this. When Canseco jumped in the air to grab a long fly hit by Cleveland Indian Carlos Martinez in the fourth inning, the ball didn't land in his glove. It bounced off his head and went over the wall. The Indians were 7–6 winners, thanks to Canseco's noggin.

Most home runs by a player in a professional baseball season (pre-Barry Bonds)

72: Joe Bauman, Roswell (class C), 1956

Most people know Roswell, New Mexico, for the alleged UFO crash there in 1947. But baseball fans may not know that it was also the home of baseball's pre-Barry Bonds home-run king. Slugger Joe Bauman homered a record 72 times during the Roswell Rockets' 1956 class C Longhorn League season, the last dinger on September 5. Bauman finished his minor league career with a .337 average and 337 home runs, but never made it to the majors despite signing a contract with the Atlanta Braves.

Most consecutive games with a home run

8: Dale Long, Pittsburgh, 1956

8: Don Mattingly, New York (AL), 1987

8: Ken Griffey Jr., Seattle, 1993

It was the longest eight games in Dale Long's career, with the Pittsburgh Pirate hitting eight homers in eight games from May 19 to 28, 1956. Don Mattingly equaled the record of consecutive games with a homer in 1987, though the New York Yankees captain ripped 10 home runs in an eight-game span. Ken Griffey Jr.'s eight-game homer streak ended July 29, 1993 — but at least the finale was memorable. Griffey drove a double off the center-field wall.

Most home runs by a player in a month

20: Sammy Sosa, Chicago (NL), June 1998

Sammy Sosa knew how to spring into summer in June 1998. The Dominican Republic-born Chicago Cubs slugger, who was on his way to a 66-home-run season, smacked 20 taters in 30 days.

Most home runs by a player in a week

10: Frank Howard, Washington, May 12 to 18, 1968

Frank Howard would be a household name today if he had had more weeks like the one in mid-May 1968, when the Washington Senators slugger capped the most impressive week in his career in an 8–4 win over the Detroit Tigers. In 20 at-bats over six games, Howard hit 10 home runs. His eight home runs through May 17 were the most in a five-game span by any player in major league history.

Most home runs by a player in a professional game

8: Justin Clarke, Corsicana (class D), June 15, 1902

It took nine seasons in the major leagues with Cleveland, Detroit, Philadelphia, Pittsburgh and the St. Louis Browns for Justin Clarke to hit six home runs. It took just one afternoon in the Texas League for the Canadian-born Clarke to hit a record eight. They came on June 15, 1902, when Clarke achieved batting perfection in eight at-bats for the Corsicana Oil City Indians against the Texarkana Casket Makers in a 51–3 blowout in Ennis, Texas. Corsicana players homered 21 times.

Most career home runs by a player in the world

868: Sadaharu Oh

Japan exported quality cars and stereos, but not its best home-run machine. On September 3, 1977, Sadaharu Oh set a world home-run record by eclipsing Hank Aaron with his 756th. Almost a year later, on August 30, Oh reached the 800 home-run milestone by hitting a ball into a fan's shoe. Oh would finish his career in 1980 with 868 homers.

Most home runs by two teams in a game

12: Detroit vs. Chicago, May 28, 1995

On May 28, 1995, Kirk Gibson celebrated his 38th birthday in style — with a pair of home runs. Problem was, the Chicago White Sox were also hitting home runs out of Tiger Stadium, and they weren't gifts for Gibson. The White Sox beat Detroit 14–12 when the teams combined for a dozen homers. The Tigers led with seven in a losing cause.

Most home runs in a game by a single team

10: Toronto Blue Jays, September 14, 1987

Let the ornithologists decide whether the oriole or blue jay is the stronger bird. Baseball fans know the Toronto Blue Jays are tops in home-run hitting. In fact, Toronto batters cracked 10 homers against Baltimore in an 18–3 massacre in 1987. Ernie Whitt had three, while George Bell and Rance Mulliniks had a pair. Rob Ducey, Fred McGriff and Lloyd Moseby had one each.

Most home runs by two teammates in a game

6: Jeromy Burnitz and Richie Sexson, Milwaukee,
September 25, 2001

Milwaukee Brewers teammates Jeromy Burnitz and Richie Sexson had their own home-run derby going in 2001, but it ended in a 3–3 tie. What really counted was the 9–4 road win over the Arizona Diamondbacks. Burnitz's homers came in the second, fourth and sixth; Sexson's were in the fourth, sixth and ninth.

First designated hitter to hit a home run

Tony Oliva, Minnesota, April 6, 1973

Seven knee operations prevented Tony Oliva from becoming one of the game's greatest players. But the chance to be designated hitter helped him prolong an otherwise stellar career when the designated-hitter rule was introduced in 1973. (The rule allowed American League managers to substitute a non-fielding player for the pitcher in the batting order.) As the Twins' first "tenth man," Oliva was the first DH to hit a home run. He set the pace by blasting a Catfish Hunter pitch in an 8–3 win over the Oakland Athletics.

Most home runs in a season by a National League designated hitter

3: Ryan Klesko, Atlanta, 1995

There's no place like the road for Ryan Klesko. The Atlanta Braves slugger was the first player to homer in three World Series road games and is the National League's single-season home-run king for a DH. His homers came against the Cleveland Indians in Games 3, 4 and 5 of the 1995 World Series.

Most career pinch-hit home runs

20: Cliff Johnson

If you were a manager who needed punch from the pinch, your only pick was Cliff Johnson. Johnson was a reliable substitute at the plate during his 15-year career. Some players are fortunate to homer 20 times in their career. Johnson hit 20 of his 196 as a pinch-hitter.

Most home runs by a pitcher in a no-hitter

2: Rick Wise, Philadelphia (NL), June 23, 1971

The Cincinnati Reds were smarting because of Rick Wise on June 23, 1971, when the Philadelphia Phillies pitcher homered twice and allowed no hits against the Reds in a 4–0 win.

He blasted pitches by Ross Grimsley and Clay Carroll and retired Pete Rose—the future hit king—to end the game. Later that summer on August 28, Wise hit another pair of home runs, one of them a grand slam, in a 7–3 win over the San Francisco Giants.

Worst home-run hitting average

.00048: Tommy Thevenow

During his career, Babe Ruth never worried that Tommy Thevenow would challenge his home-run hitting prowess. Thevenow played 15 years for the St. Louis Cardinals, Pittsburgh Pirates, Cincinnati Reds and Boston Braves and hit two inside-the-park home runs during regular-season play—both with the 1926 St. Louis Cardinals. It's not like he didn't have his chances. He had 4,164 career at-bats.

Most consecutive inside-the-park home runs on consecutive pitches

2: Texas Rangers, August 27, 1977

They say some people have feet of clay, but New York Yankees pitcher Ken Clay had hands of clay on August 27, 1977, when the rookie allowed a pair of Texas Rangers to hit back-to-back inside-the-park home runs on consecutive pitches. Toby Harrah and Bump Wills homered in the 8–2 win over New York at Yankee Stadium.

Most at-bats without a home run, season

672: Rabbit Maranville, Pittsburgh, 1922

Maybe it was his nickname that kept Walter James Vincent "Rabbit" Maranville's hits low to the ground. The Pittsburgh Pirate made 672 at-bats in 1922, but couldn't get around the bases in one fell swoop. Maranville had just 28 home runs in 23 seasons with five teams.

Fewest home runs by a batting champion

0: Zack Wheat, Brooklyn, 1918
0: Rod Carew, Minnesota, 1972

Imagine if they had a war and nobody showed up. It's like imagining a batting champion who failed to hit a home run, though it has happened twice in baseball history. Rod Carew took the 1972 batting title without hitting a home run. He had a .318 average with the Minnesota Twins, and it was the only time in Carew's 19-year career that he went homerless. In 1918, Zack Wheat won the National League batting title without a home run. The only other time Wheat failed to hit one was during his debut 1909 season, in which he played just 26 games. Wheat's batting average: .335.

Most home runs from opposite sides of the plate in the same game, in one season, by a player who admitted to using steroids

4: Ken Caminiti, San Diego, 1996

In 1996, you could only guess where Ken Caminiti was coming from. The San Diego Padres ambidextrous hitter had dingers from both sides of the plate in the same game four times. Caminiti was the National League's most valuable player. Six years later, in 2002, he admitted to *Sports Illustrated* that steroids were the reason his 1996 season was his best.

Latest home run by innings

Harold Baines, Chicago (AL), 25th inning, May 9, 1984

Leave it to Harold Baines to put one of the longest games in major league history out of its misery. Baines is the only player to hit a home run after the 22nd inning of a major league game. His long ball—a 25th-inning homer—ended a marathon eight-hour, six-minute game between the Chicago White Sox and the visiting Milwaukee Brewers, May 9, 1984. The final score was 7–6.

The game began May 8 and went 17 innings before it was suspended at 1:05 AM, May 9, with the score tied 3–3. The teams resumed play at 6:35 PM before the scheduled evening game at Comiskey Park.

First regular-season, major league home-run hit outside the United States

Mack Jones, Montreal, April 14, 1969

Bonjour Canada. *Au revoir* baseball. Mack Jones of the Montreal Expos hit Major League Baseball's first home run in Canada on a pitch from St. Louis Cardinal Nelson Briles. It was the first inning, with two men on base and one out. The Expos won their home debut at Jarry Park 8–7.

Site of first major league, regular-season home-run hit outside North America

Tokyo, Japan, March 29, 2000

Chicago Cub Shane Andrews was the first to land a ball over the wall in the "Land of the Rising Sun." At the Tokyo Dome on March 29, 2000, he smacked a two-run homer in the seventh inning against the New York Mets to lead off 2000—the first Opening Day shot outside North America. The Cubs were 5–3 winners.

Most unrelated players named Gonzalez to hit home runs on the same day

3: May 11, 1999

They were compadres from different madres, for just one day. Juan, Luis and Alex Gonzalez—all unrelated—all hit home runs on May 11, 1999, marking a first for ballplayers with the surname Gonzalez. Luis, of the Arizona Diamondbacks, had his ninth of the season in the 10th inning off Montreal's Guillermo Mota in a 5–4 win at Phoenix. Juan Gonzalez homered in the fifth inning with two on and two out in the Florida Marlins' 5–4 win in San Diego. Alex Gonzalez stroked his eighth for Texas in the fourth inning of the Rangers' 11–5 win over the White Sox, at Comiskey Park.

Most home runs off pitchers named Bob Miller in a game

2: Don Demeter, Philadelphia, August 15, 1962

Philadelphia Phillie Don Demeter was not seeing double when he faced two Bob Millers during a 1962 game. His third- and ninth-inning blasts against the New York Mets were off two different Bob Millers. Bob (Lane) Miller surrendered Demeter's first four-bagger in the 9–3 game at the Polo Grounds. Bob (John) Miller finished the game and allowed Demeter's second homer of the game. (Bob Lane Miller was actually born Robert Lane Gemeinweiser.) Incredibly, the 1962 Mets also had a third Bob Miller on their pitching staff: Robert Gerald Miller.

First major leaguer whose first or last name begins with an "X" to hit a home run

Xavier Nady, San Diego, April 2, 2003

"X" marks the spot. San Diego Padres rookie Xavier Nady hit his first career big-league homer in 2003. It was in the fourth inning off Damian Moss in a 5–3 loss to the San Francisco Giants. Nady's home run left ex-major leaguers Xavier Hernandez and Xavier Rescigno envious. They never hit the ball and touched them all.

Only major leaguer to score a touchdown and hit a homer in the same week

Deion Sanders, New York (AL) and Atlanta (NFL), September 1989

They called him "Neon Deion," but his offensive fireworks lit up the diamond and gridiron during the same week in 1989. Deion

Sanders hit his second home run of the season for the New York Yankees in a 12–2 trampling of the Seattle Mariners at the King-dome on September 5, 1989. Just five days later, on September 10, he scored a touchdown for the National Football League's Atlanta Falcons on a punt return.

First player to hit a home run into two bodies of water
Mark Grace
They oughta call him Mark "Splash!" Grace. On May 12, 1998, while with the Chicago Cubs, Grace sent the first home-run ball into Bank One Ballpark's right-center-field swimming pool; an Arizona Diamondbacks fan swimming in the pool tossed the ball back into the outfield. Then on May 28, 2001, Grace was playing for the Diamondbacks when his 12th-inning home run beat the Giants 2–1 at Pacific Bell Park in San Francisco. The ball landed in the Pacific off McCovey Cove.

First 100 home-run hitter to run backwards around the bases
Jimmy Piersall, New York (NL), June 23, 1963
Jimmy Piersall wasn't celebrating his only National League home run by running backwards around the bases. He was just happy about hitting his 100th career major league four-bagger at Polo Grounds. Piersall had already played 17 years in the majors for the Boston Red Sox, Cleveland Indians, Washington Senators and New York Mets. His career in New York, however, was short-lived. Manager Casey Stengel released him four days after his backwards trot. Piersall ended up with the Angels in California.

Only time the Most Valuable Players from both leagues homered in the same game

June 20, 2003: Miguel Tejada, Oakland, and Barry Bonds, San Francisco

It was raining home runs by the reigning most valuable players when the San Francisco Giants and Oakland Athletics met in a 2003 interleague game. Oakland shortstop Miguel Tejada had a homer and three RBIs in the A's 5–3 win over their Bay Area rivals, while Giants leftfielder Bonds homered in his 2,500th career game. Never before had MVPs from opposite leagues—including during the World Series—cleared the fences in the same game.

First American League multiple grand slam game

May 1, 1901, Chicago vs. Detroit

It was the Herm-and-Hoy grand slam show on May 1, 1901, when Herm McFarland and Dummy Hoy of Chicago hit the first grand slams in American League history in the same game, a Chicago White Sox 19–9 win over the Detroit Tigers.

First major leaguer to hit two grand slams in a game

Tony Lazzeri, New York (al), May 24, 1936

A grand slam is a grand accomplishment. And Yankee Tony Lazzeri pulled it off twice in one game on May 24, 1936, in a 25–2 massacre of the Philadelphia Athletics.

Most grand slams in a season

6: Don Mattingly, New York (NL), 1987

They called Babe Ruth the "Sultan of Swat," but New York Yankee Don Mattingly was the "Sultan of Slam." Mattingly sure knew how to clear the bases in 1987, with six grand slams, including his last on September 29 against Boston Red Sox pitcher Bruce Hurst.

First major leaguer to hit two Opening Day
grand slams
Sixto Lezcano, Milwaukee

Grand slam-o, Sixto! The Milwaukee Brewers' Sixto Lezcano
came up big on Opening Day April 7, 1978, in an 11–3 win over
the Baltimore Orioles. Grand slam fever must have been conta-
gious that year, because teammates Gorman Thomas and Cecil
Cooper hit their own grand slams in the next two games. Two
years later, on April 10, 1980, Lezcano had a two-run shot in the
fourth and a grand slam with two out in the ninth inning of a
9–5 Brew Crew win over the Boston Red Sox.

Only player to hit a grand slam and pitch a perfect
game in the same season
Don Larsen, New York (AL), 1956

Two words best describe Don Larsen's 1956 season: "grand"
and "perfect." Larsen capped his season by throwing the only
perfect World Series game. Earlier that year, on April 22, he hit
a grand slam off Boston Red Sox pitcher Frank Sullivan to bring
home Bill Skowron, Jerry Lumpe and Andy Carey in the 13–6
Yankees win.

Least grand slams in most at-bats
One in 14,053: Pete Rose

A master of "small ball," Pete Rose hit only one
bases-clearing homer in his career. It happened on
July 18, 1964, in a 14–4 Cincinnati Reds win over
pitcher Dallas Green and his Philadelphia Phillies.
Of Rose's record 4,256 hits over 24 seasons, only
160 were homers.

First pitcher to hit a pinch-hit grand slam

Mike O'Neill, St. Louis (NL), June 3, 1902

Mike O'Neill wasn't expecting to come to the plate for the St. Louis Cardinals during a 1902 game against Boston. Nor was anyone expecting him to blast the ball over the fence. But when he did so against pitcher Togie Pittinger, he became the first big-league pitcher to hit a grand slam. The Cards won 11–9.

Only player to hit a walk-off grand slam on his birthday

Alex Rodriguez, Texas, July 27, 2002

Alex Rodriguez knows it's better to give than to receive. In 2002, the man they call A-Rod had a pair of homers on his birthday, July 27. The second was a two-out walk-off grand slam that gave his Texas Rangers a 10–6 win in the 10th inning against the Oakland Athletics.

Only canine home-run ball retrieval team

Baseball Aquatic Retrieval Korps, San Francisco

Comedian Don Novello wasn't joking when he said dogs should dive off boats in McCovey Cove and chase after balls hit over Pacific Bell Park's right-field fence. In fact, comedy became reality in 2000, when the Baseball Aquatic Retrieval Korps (BARK) was formed and Pets in Need, an animal emergency shelter and adoption service, loaned Portuguese water dogs to the San Francisco Giants for their Sunday afternoon games. The balls retrieved were sold by Pets in Need to raise money for the shelter. (And for the record, BARK's lineup was: Buoy, Georgie, Justy, Quarry, Rio, Shadow and Surfer.)

Most home runs in most stadiums
42: Fred McGriff

Fred McGriff carved another notch in his traveling bat on September 22, 2002. Not only did he become the first to hit 30 or more home runs for each of five teams, the Chicago Cub also registered a home run in his 42nd major league stadium, PNC Park in Pittsburgh. The Pirates, however, were 5–4 winners.

CHAPTER 7

Out There

PLAYING BETWEEN

THE LINES

There's a whole different world out there on the field and on the base paths. There's a 450-foot trail, three bags and three corners, an expansive outfield with daunting foul territories and a collection of unusual characters. Watch where you step!

Pettiest reason for a dispute among infielders

Missed taxi ride

Joe Tinker to Johnny Evers to Frank Chance. It was baseball's greatest double-play combination, but two-thirds of the Chicago Cubs infielding trio wouldn't speak to each other for the better part of 25 years. On September 14, 1905, shortstop Tinker and second baseman Evers slugged each other during an exhibition game in Washington, Indiana, after Evers hopped in a taxicab and left his teammates behind at the hotel. Tinker and Evers made peace during a chance meeting at a Chicago radio station in 1930.

Most gracious fielder

Cal Ripken Jr., Baltimore

Legendary shortstop and third baseman Cal Ripken Jr. had played 2,632 consecutive games—and could have made it 2,633 on September 20, 1998. He was fit and ready to go, but asked Orioles manager Ray Miller to give someone else a chance to play. That someone was Ryan Minor, who went 1- for 4 in the 5–4 loss to the Yankees. Ripken had already surpassed Lou Gehrig's 2,130 straight major league games and Sachio Kinugasa's world record of 2,216. It was the first time Ripken sat out a game since he debuted as a pinch-runner on August 10, 1981.

Most positions played in a game

9: Bert Campaneris, Cesar Tovar and Scott Sheldon

You might call Bert Campaneris a "Bert of all trades." Campaneris took a tour around the ballpark for the Kansas City Athletics on September 8, 1965, when he played every position against the California Angels in a 5–3, 13-inning loss. Campaneris even allowed a hit and two walks and made a strikeout during his tenure on the mound. Three years later on September 22, 1968, Campaneris's cousin, Cesar Tovar, equaled the record for the Minnesota Twins in a

2–1 win. It took almost 32 years for another player to match the feat. This time it was Texas Ranger Scott Sheldon in a 13–1 loss to the host Chicago White Sox on September 6, 2000.

Longest-running double-play duo
Lou Whitaker and Alan Trammell, Detroit
The Detroit Tigers have a lot of individual greats: Ty Cobb, Al Kaline and Charlie Gehringer, to name a few. But not until September 9, 1977, did they have a truly dynamic duo. That was the day shortstop Alan Trammell and second baseman Lou Whitaker debuted. The pair played together for 1,198 games, including the Tigers' 1984 World Series championship.

First expansion team player to end his career on a triple play
Joe Pignatano, New York (NL), September 30, 1962
Trust the 1962 New York Mets to find innovative ways to kill a rally. Joe Pignatano had the honors of hitting into a triple play to end the eighth inning of a 5–1 loss to the Chicago Cubs. It turned out to be the Mets catcher's final trip to the plate of his six-year, five-team career. It was also the Mets' record 120th loss of the season.

Most famous catch by an outfielder
Willie Mays, New York (NL), 1954 World Series
Willie Mays made a record 7,095 putouts, but the only one everyone remembers—even if they weren't alive to see it—is his Game 1 catch of the World Series at the Polo Grounds in New York, September 29, 1954. In any other park, Cleveland's Vic Wertz would have been celebrating a homer, but centerfielder Mays gloved the 460-foot shot by Wertz in deep center during the eighth inning. The score remained tied 2–2 until the 10th, when Dusty Rhodes hit a three-run homer for the 5–2 Giants win.

Most runners left on base

45: Kansas City vs. Texas, June 16, 1991
45: New York (NL) vs. St. Louis, September 11, 1974
There's no place like home, but don't tell that to all the players
who were stranded on the bases during an 18-inning marathon in
1991. The Kansas City Royals and Texas Rangers stranded 25 and
20 base runners, respectively, as the Royals won 4–3. The New
York Mets and St. Louis Cardinals did the same in 1974 during a
25-inning, 4–3 Cards win.

Most triple steals in a game

2: Philadelphia (AL), July 25, 1930
Attention Cleveland Indians fielders: pay attention! In
1930, the Philadelphia Athletics took advantage of the
Indians with a pair of successful triple steals in a
14–1 win. In the first inning, Al Simmons, Bing Miller and
Dib Williams advanced simultaneously. Mickey Cochrane,
Simmons and Jimmie Foxx did it in the fourth.

Sneakiest baserunner

Ty Cobb, Detroit
Never turn your back on Ty Cobb. On May 12, 1911, Cobb scored
the winning run in grand fashion. He had just doubled home a
pair of runs in the seventh inning to tie the visiting New York
Yankees at Detroit's Bennett Park, when Yankee catcher Ed
Sweeney disputed the umpire's safe call. As Cobb got comfortable
at second base, other Yankee infielders joined Sweeney to state
their case. Meanwhile, Cobb ambled to third base and then sped
home for the 6–5 winning run.

Most consecutive stolen bases
50: Vince Coleman, St. Louis, 1988–1989
Without question, Vince Coleman was the fastest man in baseball. Although the game is not clocked, there are records that will confirm Coleman's fleet feet, which helped him steal a record 50 bases in a row for St. Louis from September 18, 1988, to July 26, 1989.

First ex-convict to lead both leagues in basestealing
Ron LeFlore
When he was a teenager, Ron LeFlore compiled an unsavory record for stealing that often landed him in court and jail. But in baseball, the Detroit native was honored when he set records as the first two-league thief. He was the American League's top basestealer in 1978, with 68 for the Detroit Tigers. Two years later, he won the 1980 National League race with 97 while playing for the Montreal Expos. LeFlore had taken advantage of a two-day pass from jail in June 1973 to try out for the Tigers. A year later he was a free man playing major league baseball.

Only players to steal a base in four different decades
Ted Williams, Rickey Henderson and Tim Raines Sr.
Once a thief, four decades a thief. Ted Williams stole just 24 bases in a career that spanned 1939 to 1960. But he got two as a rookie and one in the final campaign of his four-decade career. Rickey Henderson and Tim Raines Sr. both stole bases in the 1970s, 1980s, 1990s and 2000s. Henderson recorded 1,305, while Raines had 808.

Baseball's only designated runner
Herb Washington, Oakland, 1974
Herb Washington never picked up a bat or fielder's glove during his

two-year career as baseball's only full-time designated runner. Washington was a sprinter from Michigan State University who ran the 60-yard dash in a world record 5.8 seconds. Athletics owner Charlie Finley signed him, but Washington was successful only 31 times on 48 stolen base attempts after he debuted on April 4, 1974.

Costliest baserunning mistake

Fred Merkle, New York (NL), September 23, 1908

New York Giants first baseman Fred Merkle would never run to the clubhouse again. His premature exit from the field in 1908 cost his team the National League pennant. Merkle didn't touch second base in that September 23 game because he believed Moose McCormick had already scored on Al Bridwell's tie-breaking single. But Chicago Cubs second baseman Johnny Evers successfully complained to umpire Hank O'Day, and National League officials declared the game a 1–1 tie and forced an October 8 replay. The Cubs doubled the Giants 4–2 to take the pennant and later beat the Detroit Tigers for the first back-to-back World Series championships.

Most switch-hitters in an infield

5: Los Angeles Dodgers, 1965–1966

From 1965 to 1966, the Los Angeles Dodgers' infield included an all-switch-hitting lineup with first baseman Wes Parker, second baseman Jim Lefebvre, shortstop Maury Wills and third baseman Junior Gilliam.

Team with the longest-running infield

Los Angeles Dodgers, 1973–1981

The infield at Chavez Ravine of second baseman Davey Lopes, third baseman Ron Cey, shortstop Bill Russell and first baseman Steve Garvey was together for nine seasons.

First all-Johnson play

July 8, 1934

First names were mandatory for the radio play-by-play announcers during a 1934 game between the Philadelphia Athletics and Boston Red Sox. Bob Johnson of the Athletics hit Boston pitcher Hank Johnson's offering to center field. Roy Johnson was there to make the out for the Red Sox.

Most errors by one team in a game, post-1900

12: Detroit Tigers, 1901
12: Chicago White Sox, 1903

You've heard of baseball's hit parade. Well, how about the miss parade? On May 1, 1901, the Chicago White Sox took advantage of a record 12 Detroit Tiger errors in a 19–9 win. The Tigers recorded 10 errors by infielders. The White Sox tied the record against the Tigers on May 6, 1903.

Most individual errors in an inning

4: Lew Whistler, Jimmy Burke, Bob Brenly

Beware the fourth inning! Four errors await those who are cursed. New York Giant Lew Whistler, Milwaukee Brewer Jimmy Burke and San Francisco Giant Bob Brenly all recorded a quartet in the fourth. But Brenly did something the other two didn't when they set their dubious records in 1891 and 1901, respectively. He salvaged the game—and his reputation—with four RBIs. On September 14, 1986, when the San Francisco Giants catcher was playing third base, he had a pair of solo home runs and a two-run single to turn a 4–0 loss into a 7–6 victory over the Atlanta Braves.

First team to field an all non-white lineup

Pittsburgh Pirates, September 1, 1971

Pittsburgh Pirates manager Danny Murtaugh said he was "color blind" when he fielded the first non-white lineup in major league history on the first day of September, 1971. For the record, the batting order was: second baseman Rennie Stennett, centerfielder Gene Clines, rightfielder Roberto Clemente, leftfielder Willie Stargell, catcher Manny Sanguillen, third baseman Dave Cash, first baseman Al Oliver, shortstop Jackie Hernandez and pitcher Dock Ellis. Pittsburgh beat the visiting Phillies 10–7.

Most rookies in a major league starting lineup
9: Houston Colt .45s, September 27, 1963

Houston Colt .45s manager Harry Craft tried something clever when his team reached the end of its sophomore National League season. Craft wanted to give fans a taste of the future with an all-rookie lineup against the New York Mets. The starting lineup: leftfielder Brock Davis, centerfielder Jimmy Wynn, rightfielder Aaron Pointer, first baseman Rusty Staub, second baseman Joe Morgan, third baseman Glenn Vaughan, shortstop Sonny Jackson, catcher Jerry Grote and pitcher Jay Dahl. But the experiment failed in a 10–3 loss to the visitors. Less than two years later, Dahl was killed in a car accident at age 19. He had the tragic distinction of being the only player with major league experience to die in his teens.

First player beaned with a cellphone
Carl Everett, Texas, April 19, 2003

It was a call that Texas Rangers rightfielder Carl Everett never chose to take, when he was struck in the back of the head by a cellphone tossed by a fan during a 12–2 loss to the Oakland Athletics. The incident happened before the start of the sixth inning in Oakland's Network Associates Coliseum. Everett threw the phone back over the fence into a stairwell, where it hit A's employee Daniel Sugayan (who was not injured). A's rightfielder Terrence Long found the phone's battery lying on the field when he took his place in the top of the sixth. A 24-year-old man from Palo Alto, California, was charged with assault with a deadly weapon for throwing the phone from the second deck.

First major leaguer to blow a ball foul
Lenny Randle, Seattle, May 27, 1981

Lenny Randle was trying to strike a blow against the Kansas City Royals at Seattle's Kingdome. So after Royal Amos Otis hit a grounder along the third-base line, he got on his hands and knees and tried forcing the ball to go foul by blowing at it. Home-plate umpire Larry McCoy deemed the ball foul, until Kansas City manager Jim Frey argued that Randle's actions were illegal. Randle later denied blowing air at the ball; he claimed to have been yelling, "Go foul! Go foul!" The Mariners lost 8–5 to the Royals.

Only fan arrested for giving a player her phone number during a game
Kristilee Wilcox

Kristilee Wilcox was a New York City department store employee arrested on the job for missing a July 2002 court date. Her crime? Jumping on-field at Yankee Stadium during the home opener on April 16, 2002, to give shortstop heartthrob Derek Jeter her phone number. Wilcox took off her shoes but not her socks; she wanted them to collect some dirt from the famous stadium's diamond. Jeter was 2-for-5 with a stolen base, but the Baltimore Orioles won 5–4.

First baseman with the most convictions for growing marijuana

Ferris Fain: 2

When his playing days were over, Ferris Fain got into a different kind of fielding. Until 1955, the first baseman from San Antonio, Texas, who was nicknamed "Burrhead," played nine years for the Philadelphia Athletics, Chicago White Sox, Detroit Tigers and Cleveland Indians. Fain finally retired to El Dorado County, California, where he farmed—until police raided his barn in September 1985 and found his marijuana plants. After a plea bargain, Fain got four months house arrest, five years probation and a $7,500 fine for growing pot. Police returned on March 17, 1988, and again found Fain flouting the law—with a hydroponic grow operation. The cops seized 400 plants for a total of $1 million worth of pot. Fain spent 18 months in Vacaville state prison for growing and possessing marijuana for the purpose of sale.

Longest affair with a third baseman—exposed in a men's magazine

4 years: Wade Boggs and Margo Adams

Boston Red Sox third baseman Wade Boggs couldn't help going beyond third base with a woman who wasn't his wife. When his mistress, Margo Adams, detailed their affair in the April 1989 edition of *Penthouse* (she was paid $100,000 for the tell-all), the magazine's cover read: "Baseball's sexiest secret is out! Exclusive: Margo Adams vs. Wade Boggs—baseball's biggest bust-up." Adams was a mortgage broker from Santa Ana, California, who traveled with Boggs from 1984 to 1988. Boggs said the affair was a four-year "addiction" to sex, though it didn't lead to divorce. His wife, Debbie, with whom he lived in Florida, forgave him.

Only fielder to tag out a nightclub lounge singer

Paul Dean, Cincinnati, July 31, 1935

There was an overflow crowd at Cincinnati's Crosley Field for the game, July 31, 1935. So much so that fans were allowed to stand at field level. One of them was Kitty Burke, a nightclub lounge singer. Never bashful, Burke picked up Babe Herman's bat and, wearing high-heel shoes, approached the plate at the start of the eighth inning to connect with Paul Dean's pitch, which she sent rolling down the first-base line. Much to Dean's pleasure, he got the ball and tagged her out at first.

Only shortstop whose initials were also his first name

U.L. Washington

It was Un-Likely, but true. U.L. Washington was an 11-year major leaguer with the Kansas City Royals, Montreal Expos and Pittsburgh Pirates who was known simply as U.L. — and nothing else. The initials *were* his first name.

First ball girls in major league baseball

Sheryl Lawrence and Debbi Sivyer, Oakland, 1971

Baseball always had bat boys — and no ball girls. But all that changed when Oakland Athletics owner Charlie Finley hired Sheryl Lawrence and Debbi Sivyer to sit at field level and retrieve foul balls during home games in 1971. Umpires were most fond of Sivyer, who also delivered homemade cookies and lemonade to them during games. In fact, the cookies became Sivyer's life when, in 1977, she started a chain of cookie stores called Mrs. Fields Company.

First ball girl fired for posing nude
Marla Collins, Chicago (NL), 1986
Chicago is the corporate hometown of *Playboy* magazine,
and the city where Marla Collins worked as a ball girl
until the Cubs fired her on July 22, 1986, for appearing
nude in the magazine. The photo feature in the September 1986 edition included Collins in (and out of) her
Cubs uniform. No players were in the photos, but play-
by-play man Harry Caray was. He remained clothed for
the shoot and kept his job. Collins's Wrigley Field stats:
1982–1986.

Only outfielder who claimed to be a laborer found nude in a vehicle by police
Cleon Jones, New York (NL), 1975
When police found Cleon Jones in St. Petersburg, Florida, on
May 4, 1975, they thought they were dealing with a laborer who
had forgotten his clothes. They eventually realized they were
looking at a major league baseball player. Jones was found in a
van with a teenage girl who was holding drugs, an incident that
earned Jones his release from the New York Mets for "insubor-
dination." Jones wound up his 13-year career in 1976 with the
Chicago White Sox.

Only rookie fielder on probation due to rape allegations
Jim Rivera, Chicago (AL), 1952
You're innocent until proven guilty, unless you're a baseball player
accused of rape, it seems. On November 12, 1952, Commissioner
Ford Frick put Chicago White Sox rookie Jim Rivera on one-year
probation. Despite a grand jury's dismissal of rape charges against

Rivera, Frick felt he had to make an example of the outfielder by taking a stand on morality.

Only outfielder put on the disabled list because of arachnophobia
Glenallen Hill, Toronto, 1990
Eight-legged creatures caused Glenallen Hill a whole lot of trouble in 1990. It all started July 6, 1990, when the Toronto Blue Jays outfielder had a nightmare about spiders attacking him. While dreaming, Hill went sleepwalking, crashed into a glass coffee table and crawled on his hands and knees through broken glass. He sustained serious cuts and could only walk on crutches. The Blue Jays put the rookie on the disabled list for 15 days, and his teammates branded him "Spiderman."

Most unusual nickname
"Death to Flying Things"
Bob "Death to Flying Things" Ferguson played in the National League in the 1880s. But the second and third baseman (who played every infield position during a 13-year pro career) preferred to be called "Old Fergie." Ferguson was a player, manager and umpire during his baseball career and presided over the National Association from 1872–1875 while still managing and playing.

CHAPTER 8

Palaces for the Fans

BALLPARK BEAUTIES

AND BEASTS

No two ballparks are the same. There are parks with green grass and blue skies, parks under a roof or removable lid to keep the rays or rains out and parks with lots of seats—because you just never know when they'll all be needed, or who will show up.

Admission charge for first ticketed baseball game

50 cents: Newtown, Long Island, July 20, 1858

Fifty cents wasn't just two bits in the mid-19th century. It was the price of admission for the 1,500 well-heeled spectators at Fashion Race Course near New York City in 1858 who watched the New York All-Stars beat Brooklyn 21–18.

Most ballparks to open on the same day

2: April 20, 1912, and April 11, 2000

April 20, 1912, was a big day in baseball history. That's when the Boston Red Sox moved into Fenway Park and beat the New York Yankees 7–6—and when Navin Field in Detroit welcomed the first Detroit Tigers game, a 6–5 win over Cleveland. These triumphs, however, were overshadowed by the sinking of the luxury cruise ship the *Titanic* in the north Atlantic off Newfoundland. On April 11, 2000, new ballparks opened in Detroit (Comerica Park) and San Francisco (Pacific Bell Park).

First team to offer beer sales

Cincinnati Red Stockings

Thirsty Cincinnati baseball fans were treated like royalty at the city's ballpark, the Palace of the Fans: in 1880, it was the first major league stadium to offer beer for sale. The National League, however, disapproved. Beer sales and the ballpark's Sunday openings earned the Red Stockings their expulsion from the league at season's end.

Baseball's first hot dog seller

Harry Stevens

Harry Stevens was baseball's greatest purveyor of hot dogs, though they were called frankfurters at the time. It wasn't until a newspaper cartoon compared the tube steaks to dachshunds—

Theodore Dorgan's December 12, 1906, caricature—that they became forever known as hot dogs. Stevens, who hawked score-cards at baseball games in the 1880s, added food, beer, soft drinks, peanuts and cigars to his menu before the turn of the century at New York's Polo Grounds. Stevens died in 1934, but his grandsons continued to operate his empire. They later had contracts with Houston's Astrodome, Boston's Fenway Park and New York's Shea Stadium. The company Stevens started was later bought out by the conglomerate Aramark.

First use of a protective field tarp

Exposition Park, Pittsburgh, May 6, 1906

A canvas covering the infield prevented rain from ruining games at Exposition Park in 1906, but it didn't stop the visiting Cubs from beating the Pirates 5–1 the first time it was used. Today, every ball-park exposed to the elements has a tarp to prevent soggy infields.

Worst stadium collapse

Baker Bowl, Philadelphia, August 6, 1903

Investigators weren't sure what the distraction was outside the 1903 game between the Philadelphia Phillies and Brooklyn Superbas, but they knew it was fatal—after hundreds of fans inside Baker Bowl went to check out the commotion on August 6 and the bleachers collapsed under the weight. A dozen people died and 232 were injured.

First man to activate the lights for a major league game

Larry MacPhail, May 24, 1935

It's not unusual for American presidents to attend baseball games and toss the ceremonial opening pitch. But President Franklin Roosevelt had a different task the night the Cincinnati Reds hosted the first major league game under lights—to ignite the

Crosley Field floodlights from the comfort of the White House. (Roosevelt pushed the Western Union telegraph key at 8:30 PM, though that was just a signal for Reds general manager Larry MacPhail to flip the light switch from a field-level table.) The 632 lights bathed the 20,422 fans in artificial sun as they watched their Reds edge the Philadelphia Phillies 2–1.

Last major league ballpark to install lights

Wrigley Field, August 8, 1988

It's called the "Friendly Confines." But until August 1988, it was the unlit confines, and purists wanted to keep Chicago's Wrigley Field that way. (Historians note that Cubs owner Philip K. Wrigley was planning to install lights as early as the 1942 season but donated the equipment to the war effort after the Japanese air force bombed Pearl Harbor.) The park was finally illuminated on August 8, 1988, though the historic match with the Philadelphia Phillies lasted just three and a half innings because of rain. Stadium managers tried again the next night, when the Cubs beat the New York Mets 6–4.

Most expensive non-electronic scoreboard

Comiskey Park: $300,000

Bill Veeck gave baseball its first "exploding scoreboard" for the grand sum of $300,000; every time the Chicago White Sox hit a home run, the scoreboard emitted fireworks and sound effects. The first time Veeck's new scoreboard went into action was May 1, 1960, thanks to Al Smith's homer. Members of the visiting New York Yankees later poked fun at the scoreboard when they held sparklers in the air on June 17. On July 4, 1976, the exploding scoreboard was used as part of the national observations of America's Bicentennial, when the game was halted for a non-home-run fireworks display.

First female head groundskeeper

Heather Nabozny, Detroit, 1999

Diamonds are a girl's best friend. But in baseball, only one woman was a diamond's best friend: Detroit Tigers groundskeeper Heather Nabozny. The Detroit native was hired January 19, 1999, to take care of Tiger Stadium in its final season, and became Comerica Park's first groundskeeper in 2000. The graduate of Michigan State's Sports Turf Management Program got her start as a groundskeeper for the Toronto Blue Jays at their spring training facility in Dunedin, Florida, in 1993. She returned to her home state to work for the class A West Michigan Whitecaps in 1994.

First ballpark displaying metric dimensions

Jarry Park, Montreal, 1974

Canada converted to metric measurements in the 1970s, and baseball was not exempt. In 1974, the Montreal Expos' original home ballpark, Jarry Park, was the first in the major leagues to feature metric measurements on the outfield walls. For the record, the dimensions were 103.6 meters on the foul lines, 112.2 meters in the power alleys and 128 meters to straightaway center.

First major league stadium dismantled and reassembled in a foreign country

Colt Stadium, Houston

But did it have a giant "Made in the U.S.A." sticker? The original Houston National League ballpark, Colt Stadium, was used from April 10, 1962, to September 27, 1964. The Colt .45s moved indoors at the new Astrodome in 1965. The old 33,010-seat stadium stood until the 1970s, when it was taken apart, delivered to Torreon, Mexico, and rebuilt as a ballpark for a Mexican League team.

First regular-season game played indoors

April 12, 1965, Houston vs. Philadelphia

The Houston Astros must have been dazzled by their new 54,370-seat home on April 12, 1965: they lost 2–0 to the Philadelphia Phillies at the Harris County Domed Stadium, also known as the Astrodome. But the Astros did win the first exhibition game there on April 9, 1965 — 2–1 over the New York Yankees in 12 innings. (The Astrodome wasn't baseball's first covered field, however. The Negro National League's New York Cubans played under the Queensboro 59th Street Bridge during the 1930s.)

Best groundskeeper costume

The Earthmen, Houston

The uniforms worn by the Houston Astros groundskeepers were out of this world. The eight-man crew at baseball's first dome wore black combat boots, orange spacesuits and white helmets, just like astronauts — except they were dubbed the Earthmen. It was their job to take care of the Tifway Bermuda grass field under a dome the height of an 18-storey building, a job that got easier when AstroTurf was installed in 1966. Baseball's first synthetic field, custom-built for the dome by the Monsanto Company, replaced the dead grass. (All 4,596 of the stadium's translucent roof panels were painted black because outfielders complained of glare during day games.)

First game to start outside and finish inside

Chicago (NL) vs. Houston, August 11 and 26, 1966

If there had been an umbrella big enough, they would have used it in Chicago to finish a Cubs doubleheader with the Houston Astros at Wrigley Field on August 11, 1966. The second game was suspended in the seventh inning with the Astros leading 8–5. It was completed 15 days later inside Houston's Astrodome on August 26. The Astros hung on for a 9–8 win.

First major league stadium with a natural grass field under a retractable roof
Bank One Ballpark, Phoenix, 1998

De Anza zoysia isn't the name of a player, but the type of shade-tolerant grass the Arizona Diamondbacks play on at Bank One Ballpark. Phoenix's 48,700-capacity stadium hosted the first game on natural grass beneath a retractable roof on March 31, 1998, when the Colorado Rockies beat the Diamondbacks 9–2. (The roof acts as a sun shield during day games and is opened to reveal the nighttime sky above the Arizona city after dark.)

First rain-postponed game at a domed stadium
Pittsburgh vs. Houston, June 15, 1976

You've heard of a rainout. How about a rain-in? Houston's Astrodome offers protection from the oppressive heat and sub-tropical rainstorms peculiar to its part of Texas. Even when one particularly nasty weather system moved through on June 15, 1976, causing flooding in Houston's streets, the roof did its job and kept the field dry for a scheduled game between the Pittsburgh Pirates and Houston Astros. Both teams arrived and so did 20 fans, but Astros management postponed the game.

Only dome game postponed by a snowfall
California vs. Minnesota, April 14, 1983

When a heavy snowfall hit the Twin Cities in mid-April 1983, the pressure was too great on the roof of the Hubert H. Humphrey Metrodome. The snow caused a tear in the Teflon-coated fiberglass-fabric roof. The scheduled game between the Minnesota Twins and California Angels was postponed. (The heavy, wet snow that fell on the Twin Cities also prevented planes from landing at Minneapolis-St. Paul International Airport.) It was the first postponement of a game since the Twins moved indoors from Metropolitan Stadium.

Longest rainout drought

15 years: Jack Murphy Stadium, San Diego

Fans rarely needed an umbrella or rain check at Jack Murphy Stadium in San Diego. Mother Nature smiled on the Padres for a decade and a half. In fact, after the Padres' April 20, 1983, game was rained out, fans would not see another game cancelled due to the weather until May 12, 1998. That streak lasted 1,173 home dates.

Most flood-prone ballpark

Crosley Field, Cincinnati

Pitchers Gene Schott and Lee Grissom came to Crosley Field for some off-season training in a rowboat on January 27, 1937. The Cincinnati Reds ballpark was under 20 feet of water after a flood. Another flood, on April 23, 1940, postponed a game between the St. Louis Cardinals and the Reds, a first in major league history.

Only roof-tear delay in baseball history

April 26, 1986, Minneapolis

Quick, get some duct tape! As the Minnesota Twins were hosting the California Angels on April 26, 1986, high winds caused a tear in the fabric roof at the Hubert H. Humphrey Metrodome in Minneapolis. The game was delayed 15 minutes during the home half of the eighth inning. The Angels used the delay for a breather and went on to score six times in the ninth inning for a 7–6 win.

First American League game postponed
by falling roof tiles
July 19, 1994, Seattle

The sky was falling at Seattle's Kingdome on July 19, 1994, when four acoustic tiles plummeted from the ceiling before a Seattle Mariners game, forcing postponement. Tragedy struck just a few days later, when a crane broke and two workers were killed. The stadium, built for $67 million, was closed for emergency renovations at a cost of $70 million. The Mariners did not return until 1995, after the roof was fixed and the major league baseball strike resolved.

Most expensive retractable roof to get
stuck during a game
$100 million: Safeco Field

It was the longest 54 minutes in the history of the Seattle Mariners. The franchise, which played almost 24 seasons in the Kingdome, experienced its first home rain-delay July 22, 2000, when the $100-million retractable roof at Safeco Field stalled during an afternoon downpour. At 2:02 PM, third base umpire Charlie Williams called a rain delay during the game with the Texas Rangers. The roof jammed when a computer malfunctioned, so the field was covered with a silver tarp. The game resumed at 2:56 PM, and the Mariners rolled to a 13–5 victory.

First farm animal ejected from a ballpark
Goat: October 6, 1945

Wrigley Field is called the "Friendly Confines," unless you're a goat. Billy Sianis, owner of Chicago's Billy Goat Tavern, learned that the hard way during Game 4 of the 1945 World Series against the Detroit Tigers, when ushers told Sianis and his goat to take a hike. Sianis responded with the "Billy Goat hex."

Despite the Cubs' home field advantage, the Tigers took the series in seven games and the Cubs never went to another 20th-century World Series.

Most papal masses at a major league stadium

2: Yankee Stadium

Twice, the "House That Ruth Built" became a large, open-air cathedral when the spiritual leader of the world's Roman Catholics dropped in to celebrate mass. Pope Paul VI appeared on October 4, 1965, and Pope John Paul II came almost 14 years later, on October 2, 1979. Some called these visits "sermons on the mound."

First artificially colored ball field

Crosley Field, 1937

The Cincinnati Reds got tired of the sun-bleached grass in their ballpark, so they used a green dye sanctioned by the United States Green Association to bring the sod back to its emerald glory.

Highest indoor broadcast of a baseball game

208 feet, Lindsey Nelson, April 28, 1965

New York Mets play-by-play announcer Lindsey Nelson reached the zenith of his career—or at least the ceiling—on April 28, 1965, when he called the game from a gondola that was dangling from the Astrodome. The Astros were 12–9 winners.

First day-night, interleague doubleheader in different ballparks

July 8, 2000, Shea Stadium and Yankee Stadium

The New York Yankees and New York Mets met in an interleague doubleheader on July 8, 2000—but you needed tickets to two separate games in two separate stadiums to see it happen (a subway ticket didn't hurt, either). The Yankees doubled the Mets 4–2 in the day game at Shea Stadium, then repeated the score in the nightcap at Yankee Stadium.

Highest major league ballpark
Coors Field, Denver
The Colorado Rockies home ballpark in Denver is 5,176 feet above sea level.

Most expensive ballpark fountain
$3 million: Kauffman Stadium
The Kansas City Royals have a $3-million fountain called the Water Spectacular inside Kauffman Stadium. The 322-foot-wide, 10-foot-high waterfall is the centerpiece of the attraction over the outfield fence, between center field and right field.

Only island-based ballpark to host both American League and National League home games named for an ex-major league player
Hiram Bithorn Stadium, Puerto Rico
Hiram Bithorn returned to major league baseball posthumously. His name is now on the ballpark in San Juan, Puerto Rico, where the Toronto Blue Jays beat the Texas Rangers 8–1 to open the 2001 season. Two years later, the Montreal Expos played 22 "home" games there. Bithorn joined the Chicago Cubs in 1942 and spent four years in the big leagues, including a stint with the White Sox. He also spent two years in the U.S. Marine Corps during World War II. Bithorn died at age 35 when a Mexican policeman shot him on New Year's Day, 1952.

Most marijuana plants found growing in a big league park

400: Anaheim Stadium

There was a different kind of weed growing in Anaheim Stadium's outfield in early 1976, illegal weed that is. The grounds crew preparing the field for the California Angels removed some 400 marijuana plants before the Angels opened the season April 9 with a 5–2 loss to the Oakland Athletics. Nobody knows who put them there, but there were plenty of pot-smoking fans at The Who's rock concert on March 21, and groundskeepers believed the fans dropped marijuana seeds on the fertile grounds.

CHAPTER 9

Necessary Villains

UMPIRES UNMASKED

Pitcher Christy Mathewson, one of the original Hall of Fame inductees, called umpires a "necessary evil" representing order and civility (given that they uphold the rules of the game). Obviously, the best are those who are hardly noticed, though no ump is above the law and every ump makes mistakes. They are only human.

Most World Series umpired
18: Bill Klem

Bill Klem set the standard for umpires. He is even credited with saying he never missed a call, and he made a lot of calls during his 36 major league seasons behind the plate. Klem umped 104 games in 18 different World Series—including five consecutive series beginning in 1911. His first (1908) and last (1940) both featured losses by the Detroit Tigers. The Veterans Committee voted Klem into the Hall of Fame in 1953.

First umpire to work a game involving his brother
Bill Haller, July 14, 1972

There were two brothers behind the plate in the same game on July 14, 1972. Tom Haller was catching for the Detroit Tigers and went 1-for-4 in the game umpired by his brother, Bill. The Kansas City Royals won 1–0.

First father and son to ump in the same major league game
Harry and Hunter Wendelstedt, August 10, 1998

Like father, like son. Hunter Wendelstedt followed his father Harry's footsteps into a career as a major league umpire, officiating on the same crew for the first time in San Diego in 1998, when the Florida Marlins edged the Padres 3–2. Harry Wendelstedt was the home-plate umpire while Hunter was stationed at second. Hunter shifted to home plate on August 12, when the Padres beat the Braves 5–1; father Harry was at third.

Only major league umpire banned for fixing games
Dick Higham

National League umpire Dick Higham went from banned to bookmaker when, on June 24, 1882, he was found to have fixed games. Detroit Mayor William Thompson, president of the city's Wolverines ball club, grew suspicious of Higham's work and hired a private eye. The investigator found a letter Higham wrote to a bookmaker, advising him to bet on Detroit. Higham, born in Ipswich, England, played in the National Association for five years and the National League for three years .

Only major league umpire to win a Stanley Cup
Bill Stewart
Player and coach names aren't engraved on the World Series trophy, but you'll find Bill Stewart's on the Stanley Cup. The National Hockey League championship trophy belonged to the Stewart-coached Chicago Blackhawks in 1938, after they beat the Toronto Maple Leafs. Stewart, who used to referee in the NHL, was a 21-year National League umpire who umpired in four World Series.

First umpire to die at home plate
John McSherry, April 1, 1996
Cincinnati Reds owner Marge Schott was never one to mince words. She had the temerity to say, "Snow this morning and now this? I don't believe it. I feel cheated," after tragedy struck on Opening Day in Cincinnati. John McSherry, a 21-year veteran umpire, died of a heart attack at home plate only seven pitches into the first game of the season. Schott eventually apologized to the umpiring crew before the Reds hosted the Houston Astros in the second half of an April 14 doubleheader.

Most accidental career change, from player to umpire
Jocko Conlan
A damaged digit turned Jocko Conlan from a player into an umpire. Conlan, a member of the Chicago White Sox, could not

play because of a broken finger and Emmett Ormsby could not continue umpiring because of heat exhaustion. So Conlan took Ormsby's place and the 1935 game between the Browns and White Sox continued. The next season, Conlan became a minor league umpire, and eventually joined the National League in 1941. His 25-year umpiring career gained Conlan a place in the Hall of Fame.

Longest suspension for spitting at an umpire

5 games: Roberto Alomar, Baltimore, 1997

Roberto Alomar got just a slap on the wrist for spitting in the face of authority. The Baltimore Oriole spat at umpire John Hirschbeck in the first inning on September 27, 1996, after being thrown out for arguing a called third strike. Major league officials were slow to react and only suspended Alomar for the first five games of 1997. But the day after the saliva scandal, Alomar hit the game-winning 10th-inning homer to beat the Blue Jays 3–2 and secure the American League wildcard playoff berth.

First umpire to quit, manage, then ump again

George Moriarty

George Moriarty took a break from his umpiring career after 1926—not to holiday or improve his golf game, but to manage the Detroit Tigers for two seasons. During his time in the dugout, Moriarty guided the Tigers to an 82–71 record in 1927 and 68–86 in 1928. Moriarty, who earlier played third base with the Chicago Cubs, Chicago White Sox, New York Yankees and Detroit Tigers, resumed his umpiring career in 1929.

Most umpires injured on and off the field in a day

4: April 13, 1981

You didn't want to be a man in black early in 1981 in Philadelphia. At the Phillies home-opener against the Pittsburgh Pirates, home plate umpire Joe West left the game after he was struck on the head by a bat that slipped out of the hands of Phillie Lonnie Smith. Then, after the Phillies' 5–1 win, umpires Dick Stello, John Kibler and Bruce Froemming were injured in a car crash just five blocks from Veterans Stadium. Stello, the driver, suffered back and hip injuries and had to miss the last two games of the series. The National League called up minor league umps Steve Fields and Lanny Harris to replace Stello and Kibler.

Most umpires to borrow ushers uniforms

4: Art Franz, Bill Deegan, Terry Cooney and Jerry Neudecker, May 17, 1976, Memorial Stadium, Baltimore

Franz, Deegan, Cooney and Neudecker were not checking for tickets when they worked the game between the Baltimore Orioles and Milwaukee Brewers on May 17, 1976. Although dressed as ushers, they were actually the umpires. But their equipment hadn't arrived from Oakland in time, so they had to borrow black-and-orange stadium staff uniforms to officiate the 3–0 Orioles victory.

First African-American umpire
Emmett Ashford

They called Emmett Ashford the Jackie Robinson of arbiters—the majors' first black umpire when he debuted in Washington, D.C., at a Senators game on April 11, 1966. Cleveland beat the Senators 5–2 in the first game umpired by the 51-year-old.

Most clever prank by an umpire

The Easter egg incident, April 19, 1987

It was Easter Sunday 1987, and children everywhere were hunting
for hidden eggs. But Milwaukee Brewers catcher B.J. Surhoff was
only catching when he reached back for a new ball and umpire
Larry McCoy dropped an egg in his glove. Both McCoy and Surhoff
cracked up. The Brewers won 6–4 over the visiting Texas Rangers.

Most valuable apology by an umpire

George Magerkurth

On July 19, 1945, in Cincinnati, umpire George Magerkurth
assaulted a fan he mistakenly thought was heckling him. It turned
out his victim was restaurateur Thomas J. Longo of Dayton, Ohio.
When Magerkurth wrote an apology and paid Longo's $100 med-
ical bill, Longo dropped the charges.

First major league umpire jailed for a Sunday game

Tim Hurst, May 16, 1897

The Cleveland Spiders were ready to host the city's first
Sunday baseball game on May 16, 1897, but the police arrested
the players after one inning of play—even umpire Tim
Hurst was jailed. Cleveland owner Frank Robison bailed
everyone out.

Only umpire on-field for the first American League game, first World Series and first games at Shibe Park, Comiskey Park, Fenway Park and Yankee Stadium

Tom Connolly

Tom Connolly was always in the right place at the right time. He
umped the Chicago White Stockings game on April 24, 1901,
against Cleveland, and was an arbiter during the inaugural 1903
World Series. He also worked the first games at Philadelphia's

Shibe Park (April 12, 1909), Chicago's Comiskey Park (July 1, 1910), Boston's Fenway Park (April 20, 1912) and Yankee Stadium in New York (April 18, 1923).

Most temporary umpires of an extra-innings tie game
2: Jimmy Wilson and Lon Warneke, May 13, 1940
Neither the Cincinnati Reds nor the St. Louis Cardinals told league officials they were going to replay a game lost to darkness on April 23. When the teams realized they had no umpires, Reds coach Jimmy Wilson and Cards pitcher Lon Warneke became temporary arbiters while Larry Goetz, a Cincinnati-based umpire, came to relieve the men. Lucky for Johnny Mize, the game was official: he hit three home runs. But little was solved that day because the teams tied 8–8 in 14 innings, though Warneke apparently enjoyed the experience. He became an umpire and worked for the National League from 1949 to 1955.

First umpire to wear glasses in a regular-season game
Frank Umont, April 24, 1956
You wouldn't want to question Frank Umont's eyesight when he strode on-field wearing eyeglasses for the first time, to umpire a game between the Detroit Tigers and Kansas City Royals on April 24, 1956. Before umpiring, Umont played tackle and guard in the National Football League for the New York Giants.

First 21st-century attack by a fan on an umpire
April 15, 2003, Chicago
As an umpire, Laz Diaz knew verbal abuse came with the territory. But on April 15, 2003, he didn't expect to be attacked by a fan while manning first base in the eighth inning of the Chicago White Sox game with the visiting Kansas City Royals. Diaz was on his way to right field following a fly ball when the rowdy fan

tackled him. Bouncers and players rushed to his aid. The fan received a cut on the head and an assault charge. The Royals won 8–5.

First anti-video replay protest by umpires

April 17, 1977

Umpires Terry Tata, Ed Sudol, Dick Stello and Bruce Froemming didn't like being second-guessed on April 17, 1977, so they left the game and threatened not to return. Astro Bob Watson's controversial scoring play at home on a passed ball by Braves catcher Biff Pocoroba with one out in the fourth inning had been replayed on the stadium's video-replay screen. The crew walked off and only resumed work after Braves management agreed to refrain from showing similar plays on-screen. They finished the inning and the game, a 5–4 Astros win.

Longest umpiring strike

45 days: 1979

The show must go on, even without umpires, who went on strike for the first 45 days of the 1979 season. On April 24 at Shea Stadium, high school umpire Phil Lospitalier called Lee Mazzilli and Richie Heber of the New York Mets out on a double play, then returned them to the bases after Mets manager Joe Torre protested. Giants manager Joe Altobelli complained. The crew disappeared for 28 minutes to mull over their decision, then declared Mazzilli the only out on the play. On May 9, replacement umpires ejected four managers, one coach and five players throughout the majors. The striking umps finally got a new contract on May 19.

Biggest theft of a major league umpire's belongings

$17,000 in cash and valuables: Terry Tata, June 23, 1993

Wine, woman and a robbery kept umpire Terry Tata off the

job for a 1993 game in San Francisco between the Giants and San Diego Padres. The ump was found in a hotel room in Burlingame, California—the victim of a robbery. Tata claimed a woman arrived at his hotel room toting a bottle of wine. She apparently drugged him and left with $16,500 in jewelry and $500 in cash.

Most players ejected from a dugout

15: September 27, 1951

The Brooklyn Dodgers had no one left in their dugout after umpire Frank Dascoli ejected all 15 occupants in the eighth inning of a 1951 game, in which the Boston Braves were the eventual 4–3 winners. Among those tossed: minor league call-up Bill Sharman, who played for basketball's Boston Celtics in the off-season. Thanks to Dascoli's decision, the future basketball Hall of Famer never made it closer to major league action than the dugout at Ebbets Field.

Only umpire to eject an ex-football player during the seventh-inning stretch

Angel Hernandez, August 7, 2001

Was it a joke or a threat? Umpire Angel Hernandez didn't bother finding out, he just ejected Steve McMichael after the professional wrestler's comments during the seventh-inning stretch on August 7, 2001. The ex-Chicago Bears football player was unhappy with calls made against the Chicago Cubs by Hernandez. So when it came time for him to be a guest singer of "Take Me Out to the Ball Game," he told the crowd, "Don't worry, I'll have some speaks with that home-plate umpire after the game." McMichael left Wrigley Field to go to a restaurant and didn't discover he had been thrown out until he watched the end of the game on TV. The Cubs won 5–4.

Most ejections of a manager by an umpire

8: *Ron Luciano*

Baseball had its own version of the Hatfields and McCoys whenever Ron Luciano umpired a game involving the Baltimore Orioles and their tempestuous manager, Earl Weaver. Luciano ejected Weaver from games eight times—until the American League finally stopped assigning Luciano to Orioles games. The feud began during class AAA International League when Weaver managed Rochester and was ejected by Luciano the first four times they met. Luciano umpired from 1968 to 1980, authored best-selling autobiographies and was a TV commentator. He committed suicide in 1995. A year later, his nemesis, Weaver, was inducted into the Hall of Fame.

CHAPTER 10

Who's the Boss?

MANIC MANAGERS

AND COARSE COACHES

They're kind of like cats: always there, watching carefully, silently. What are they thinking? What do those hand signals mean? They're ready to pounce whenever things aren't going their way. Call them dugout bosses, skippers, men at the helm—or just plain managers.

Age of the oldest manager hired

72: Jack McKeon, Florida

Youth was not on the Florida Marlins' wish list when they went looking to replace their fired 61-year-old manager Jeff Torborg on May 10, 2003. They responded by hiring 72-year-old Jack McKeon the next day. (The only other older men to manage in the majors were Casey Stengel and Connie Mack.) McKeon celebrated with his 771st career win in his first game as Marlin manager, and guided his new team to victory in the 2003 World Series.

Age of the oldest coach

92: Jimmie Reese, California Angels

Jimmie Reese knew where to find the fountain of youth—at the ballpark. Baseball was his life, from age 15, when he was a bat boy for the Pacific Coast League's Los Angeles Angels, until age 92, as a coach with the American League's California Angels. Reese, who wore number 50 for the Angels in Anaheim, often reminisced about his three-year career as a second baseman with the St. Louis Cardinals and New York Yankees. During that time, he was a roommate with Babe Ruth. Reese died July 13, 1994.

Most years as a manager

53: Connie Mack, 1894–1896; 1901–1950

Connie Mack's 50-year tenure as manager of the Philadelphia Athletics was among the most secure in baseball history, because he also owned the team. Mack began his major league managerial career in 1894, with a three-season stint for the Pittsburgh Pirates.

Most wins and most losses

Connie Mack: 3,731 wins; 3,948 losses

You win some, you lose some. But in Connie Mack's case, he won many and lost more. Mack had the longest career of any major league manager, so it's no surprise that he amassed the most wins (3,731) and the most losses (3,948) of any manager in base-ball history.

Most years as a manager without winning a pennant
26: Gene Mauch
Gene Mauch just couldn't buy a pennant during his 26-year career managing the Philadelphia Phillies (1960–1968), Montreal Expos (1969–1975), Minnesota Twins (1976–1980) and California Angels (1981–1982, 1985–1987). His 1964 Phillies blew a seven-game lead for the National League title with 12 games left in the season. And he was equally heartbroken in 1982 and 1986, when his Angels were knocked off in the American League championship series.

Only manager of league champions in all three class-AAA leagues
Marv Foley

If class AAA baseball is a heartbeat away from the majors, then Marv Foley has been three heartbeats away from a World Series hat trick. Foley is the only manager in baseball history with the Triple-A "Triple Crown," managing the 1989 Vancouver Canadians to the Pacific Coast League championship, the Iowa Cubs to the 1993 American Association championship and the Rochester Red Wings to the 1997 International League championship. But Foley never duplicated his minor league triumphs in the majors. He played parts of four seasons with the Chicago White Sox until a single season with the Texas Rangers in 1984, then saw some coaching action for the Chicago Cubs in 1994.

Only manager of a major league team to coach college football and National Football League teams

Hugo Bezdek

Hugo Bezdek was a Czech who bounced from Major League Baseball into college and pro football. The Pittsburgh Pirates promoted the native of Prague from west coast scout to manager in 1917, where he lasted until 1919 and compiled a 166–187 record as a Major League Baseball manager. His first love, however, was football. The Cleveland Rams of the National Football League hired him in 1937, but fired him a year later after the team went 1–13. Bezdek returned to college football where his teams in Oregon, Arkansas and Pennsylvania gave him a 124–54–16 record.

Hardest manager to eject

Connie Mack

An umpire never ejected Connie Mack from a game. Maybe it was because of his stately appearance. Mack, the "Tall Tactician," was six feet, 150 pounds and never wore a uniform like his players. Instead, he preferred a three-piece suit, tie and fedora or derby hat.

Most teams managed

7: Frank Bancroft

Frank Bancroft was a nomad among baseball managers. During his nine-year major league career between 1880 and 1902, Bancroft managed seven teams: Worcester and the Detroit Wolverines, Cleveland Spiders, Providence Grays, Indianapolis Hoosiers and Cincinnati Reds of the National League and the Philadelphia Athletics of the American Association. Bancroft's only pennant win was with the 1884 Providence Grays. The 84–28 Grays took on the New York Metropolitans of the American Association and achieved a three-game sweep during the October 23 to 25 series. Bancroft retired in 1902 with a 375–333 record.

Most managers of a team in one game

1,115: St. Louis Browns, August 24, 1951

Democracy ruled at Sportsman's Park in St. Louis when Browns owner Bill Veeck offered his fans the chance to manage the team for a day. During a 1951 game against the Philadelphia Athletics, 1,115 people were given "Yes" and "No" flash cards, and when asked by the public address announcer, offered their opinion on strategy. Manager Zack Taylor put the will of the fans into action and the Browns were 5–3 winners. Perhaps Veeck should have employed the strategy more often. Taylor compiled a disappointing 52–102 record for eighth place in the American League.

Biggest coaching failure

The Chicago Cubs' "College of Coaches"

The Chicago Cubs had a revolving door in the manager's office during 1961 to 1965, when they didn't have a single full-time manager. Instead, the team employed baseball's first—and last—college of coaches. Six men took turns managing the team, but none graduated with a record of .500 or better, including Vedie Himsl (1961), Harry Craft (1961), Elvin Tappe (1961–1962), Lou Klein (1961–1962, 1965), Charlie Metro (1962) and Bob Kennedy (1963–1965). Kennedy served the longest with a 182–198 record and .479 winning percentage. Craft had the shortest tenure, going 7–9.

Biggest managerial gambling scandal

Tris Speaker and Ty Cobb

Tsk, tsk, Tris and Ty. A gambling scandal almost ended the careers of two of the game's greatest players when, on November 29, 1926, Tris Speaker quit his job as Cleveland Indians manager. Commissioner Kenesaw Mountain Landis called Speaker and Ty Cobb into a closed-door meeting with Joe Wood, a retired pitcher and outfielder, and Wood and Cobb were accused of betting on the game between the Detroit Tigers and Cleveland Indians held September 25, 1919. Ex-Tigers pitcher Dutch Leonard claimed, in writing, that Cobb and Speaker agreed to throw the game so that the Tigers would win third-place prize money. But Leonard did not appear at the hearings conducted by Landis on January 5, 1927, so Cobb and Speaker were cleared and reinstated. Cobb joined Connie Mack's Philadelphia Athletics on February 8, while Speaker signed with the Washington Senators on January 31.

Biggest suspension for enlarging the batter's box
$500: Maury Wills, Seattle, April 25, 1981
Maury, Maury, say you're sorry! Seattle Mariners manager Maury Wills asked the Kingdome grounds crew to make the batter's box one foot closer to the mound, so that it would be easier for Mariners pitchers to strike out Oakland Athletics batters. Billy Martin noticed the bigger box before the game and told umpire Bill Kunkel. Kunkel measured the box at seven feet long; it should have been six. Wills was suspended two games and fined $500. The Athletics beat the Mariners 7–4.

Biggest pro-smoking protest by a manager
Earl Weaver, 1969
Earl Weaver didn't like what umpires told him. That was especially true the day he was thrown out of a 1969 game before it even started for smoking a cigarette in the dugout. The Baltimore Orioles skipper protested umpire Frank Umont's decision the next day by handing in his team's lineup with a cigarette in his mouth. Of course, 1969 was the year the O's smoked in the regular season with 109 wins and then got smoked in the World Series by New York's "Miracle Mets."

Biggest animal given to a manager by a player

Hereford cow

As a surprise, Seattle Mariner Ken Griffey Jr. "moo-ved" a pregnant, 1,200-pound Hereford cow into manager Lou Piniella's office in Peoria, Arizona, on March 15, 1995. Piniella had earlier won a bet with Griffey on whether he could hit a batting practice pitch out of the cage. The prize was a steak dinner, but Griffey took it to the extreme. Piniella later joked with reporters that "Bo Vine" would play in center field instead of Griffey during a spring training game.

Worst managerial record by a team owner

0–1: Ted Turner, Atlanta, May 1, 1977

Some say Ted Turner is a legend in his own mind. When his Atlanta Braves lost 16 straight games in May 1977, he had a replacement in mind for manager Dave Bristol: himself (though instead of firing Bristol, he sent him on a scouting trip). Turner's only game at the helm was a 2–1 loss to the Pittsburgh Pirates on May 1, 1977. National League president Chub Feeney vetoed a second appearance for Turner, reminding him that a manager could not own shares in a team. Suffice to say, Turner did not choose the "sell" option. Turner was not the first Braves owner to manage the team, however. In 1929, Emil Fuchs had a 56–98 record in Boston.

Most times fired by the same owner

5: Billy Martin, New York (AL)

New York Yankees fans loved Billy Martin for his playing heroics, which earned him Most Valuable Player honors of the 1953 World Series. When he became a manager, relations were less cordial with owner George Steinbrenner, who fired Martin a record five times. Martin kept coming back because he had led the team to its first World Series win of the decade in 1977. His last tour of duty with the Yankees was in June 1988.

Most desperate coach to end a slump

Rich Donnelly, Texas, August 3, 1983

Peggy Donnelly had an asinine idea to lift the Texas Rangers out of a slump. The Rangers had lost 21 of 26 games when the wife of first-base coach Rich Donnelly painted TR—the team's initials—in block letters on her husband's bottom. During a team meeting, Donnelly went into manager Doug Rader's office and emerged wearing only a sweater, then chanted "V-I-C-T-O-R-Y!" before flashing his behind at the players. It didn't work. The Rangers lost 5–4 in 10 innings at home to the Boston Red Sox.

First rookie manager targeted with clown harassment

Bob Melvin, Seattle

Seattle Mariners rookie manager Bob Melvin didn't like to clown around. In fact, he was afraid of clowns. That's one of the secrets the former Arizona Diamondbacks coach told manager Bob Brenly and coaches Tony Dello and Robin Yount. So the trio hired two clowns—named Bob and Melvin—to walk around Tucson Electric Park and taunt Melvin when he brought the Mariners to the field for a spring training game on March 11, 2003.

First manager fired for lying about his service in the Vietnam War

Tim Johnson, Toronto

Toronto Blue Jays manager Tim Johnson went from alleged hero to certified zero. Johnson guided the Blue Jays to a third-place 88–74 record in the American League East division in 1998. He tried to inspire his players to win with heroic tales of his battles for the United States Marine Corps in the Vietnam War. But the truth was that Johnson had only trained Vietnam-bound recruits; he never served in Southeast Asia. Johnson eventually apologized to his players for lying, but it was too late. He was fired on March 18, 1999, and replaced by Jim Fregosi after only three wins in 15 spring training games.

First manager ejected from both halves of a doubleheader

Earl Weaver, Baltimore, August 15, 1975

The score was Ron Luciano 2, Earl Weaver 0, when umpire Luciano tossed Baltimore Orioles boss Weaver twice in one night during a 1975 doubleheader. Weaver argued a call by Luciano in the top of the fourth inning of the first game, a 10–6 loss to the Texas Rangers, by piling dirt atop first base. Before the second game, Weaver began an argument with Luciano while exchanging lineup cards. The Orioles did better without their leader: they were 13–1 winners of the nightcap.

First manager to forget his team's name on the day he is hired

Casey Stengel, New York (NL), September 16, 1961

Casey Stengel was always good for a quip. But when he was introduced to the press as the New York Mets' first manager, Stengel said he was glad to be managing again and called the National League expansion team "the Knickerbockers." That's the long name for the city's National Basketball Association team, the Knicks.

First manager and broadcaster switch

Lou Boudreau for Charlie Grimm, Chicago (NL)

Charlie Grimm was called up and Lou Boudreau was sent down on May 4, 1960. But not to the minors. Instead, Boudreau returned to managing the Chicago Cubs after just 17 games as a color commentator on WGN Radio. Boudreau replaced Grimm, who found a new job behind Boudreau's microphone.

Most bizarre trade

Joe Gordon for Jimmy Dykes

Some teams will pay a high price for a pitcher or slugger to help them get back on the winning track. But on August 3, 1960, the Cleveland Indians and Detroit Tigers chose a different strategy: they swapped managers. The Indians sent Joe Gordon to Detroit for Jimmy Dykes in a deal conceived by Detroit general manager Bill DeWitt. It was a convenient trade for Indians general manager Frank "Trader" Lane, who reluctantly signed Gordon to a two-year contract. Gordon wanted to leave the Indians after the 1959 season, but Lane failed to sign replacement Leo Durocher.

Worst injury in an assault by a player

Shattered cheekbone: Frank Lucchesi, Texas

Lenny Randle flew off the handle on March 28, 1977. The raging Texas Rangers second baseman didn't like it when he found out manager Frank Lucchesi had called him a "punk" in front of reporters. He approached Lucchesi from behind a batting cage at the Rangers spring training facility in Orlando, Florida, and, with Lucchesi's hands in his pockets, let the punches fly, shattering Lucchesi's right cheekbone. The manager needed plastic surgery to repair his face. Randle could have been jailed for up to 15 years, but instead he was fined

$1,000 by a judge and ordered to pay Lucchesi's medical bills.
The Rangers also levied a fine against Randle ($10,000), then
released him after a month's suspension.

Most stitches required to mend a Billy Martin assault victim

15: Joseph Cooper, October 23, 1979

Joseph Cooper was the world's most famous marshmallow sales-
man after Billy Martin assaulted him in a Minneapolis bar.
Cooper and Martin were arguing about baseball when Martin
punched out the 52-year-old Cooper, who needed 15 stitches to
mend his split lip. New York Yankees owner George Steinbrenner
fired Martin after the altercation.

First native New Yorker to manage the New York Yankees

Joe Torre

Joe Torre was born July 18, 1940, in Brooklyn, but he is best
known for what he did in the Bronx. Torre is the only manager
in the team's history who was born in one of the Big Apple's five
boroughs. Torre, who joined the Yankees in 1996 and led them
to four World Series championships, got his start managing in
the borough of Queens with the New York Mets, 1977 to 1981.

Most unusual birthday gift for a manager

Black sheep: Napoleon Lajoie

Cleveland Indians fans were a wild and woolly bunch. They
celebrated manager Napoleon Lajoie's birthday on September 5, 1907, by showering him with gifts, including a
live black sheep.

First manager interviewed on television

Connie Mack, Philadelphia (AL), February 11, 1937

Connie Mack made TV history in a place where televisions were made. The legendary Philadelphia Athletics manager was interviewed during a live broadcast from a Philco television factory to demonstrate the new technology.

First African-American major league coach

Buck O'Neil, Chicago (NL), 1962

John "Buck" O'Neil may have been the best major league manager who never was. The Negro Leagues' fielding star managed the Kansas City Monarchs to five pennants and two Negro League championships between 1948 and 1955, but never got a chance to manage in the majors. The closest he came was coaching with the Chicago Cubs from 1962 to 1965.

First African-American major league manager

Frank Robinson, Cleveland, 1975

Frank Robinson blasted his way through the color barrier when he debuted as manager of the Cleveland Indians on April 8, 1975, then put himself in the lineup as designated hitter. His record eighth Opening Day homer keyed the Indians' 5–3 win over the New York Yankees. Robinson went on to manage in San Francisco, Baltimore and Montreal.

Second African-American manager

Larry Doby, Chicago (AL), 1978

Larry Doby was always number two. In 1947, he was the second black man to play 20th-century major league baseball after Jackie Robinson. He took over the Chicago White Sox from Bob Lemon on June 30, 1978, and became baseball's second African-American manager.

Most World Series ejections of a manager

2: Bobby Cox, Atlanta

When Bobby Cox lost his temper in the World Series, his team also lost the championship. Cox was tossed from Game 6 of the 1996 World Series on October 26, 1996, when third-base umpire Tim Welke showed the Atlanta Braves manager the exit in the fifth inning. Cox had just finished arguing with second-base umpire Terry Tata over his decision to call Marquis Grissom out at second, then swore at Welke as he walked to the dugout. The Yankees were 3–2 winners of the game and 4–2 winners of the series. Cox's first World Series ejection was Game 3 of the 1992 World Series against the Toronto Blue Jays. The Braves also lost that game 3–2 and that series 4–2.

Only pitcher to work under seven managers in a season

Dock Ellis, 1977

Dock Ellis needed a scorecard of his own to keep track of who his manager was during 1977. He appeared in games for Billy Martin's New York Yankees, Jack McKeon and Bobby Winkles's Oakland Athletics and the Texas Rangers, who used four managers. The men who came and went in Arlington, Texas, that season were Frank Lucchesi, Eddie Stanky, Connie Ryan and Billy Hunter.

Biggest fine for a manager appearing in a beer ad

$500: Casey Stengel, April 24, 1962

When the New York Mets won their first game on April 23, 1962, a 9–1 decision over the Pittsburgh Pirates at Forbes Field, manager Casey Stengel celebrated with a cold one. He appeared in uniform in an ad for Rheingold Beer with the Miss Rheingold pageant winner. Commissioner Ford Frick poured Stengel a $500 fine.

Worst injury suffered by a batting coach heading to batting practice

Jack Clark, Los Angeles, March 31, 2003

Jack Clark wore a helmet during his 18-year major league career, but wasn't wearing one while riding his motorcycle to Bank One Ballpark in Phoenix. The Los Angeles Dodgers batting coach suffered eight broken ribs and cuts to his head and face when a minivan driver made an unsafe lane change and hit a car, which struck Clark's motorcycle.

Most coaches ejected after throwing candy and gum on the field

2: Lee Elia and John McLaren, Tampa Bay, August 31, 2003

When snacks and sweets landed outside the Devil Rays dugout in Oakland, third-base umpire Derryl Cousins automatically suspected the hot-tempered Lou Piniella. But "Sweet Lou" was innocent, for once. McLaren, the bench coach, and Elia, the hitting coach, were protesting a walk given Athletics catcher Ramon Hernandez by umpire Joe Brinkman after a check swing. Hernandez and two other A's scored on Frank Menechino's single for a 4–3 win.

Most embarrassing moment for a retired manager

Public nudity: Dick Williams, January 17, 2000

Citizens in Fort Myers, Florida, saw too much Dick on January 17, 2000 — Dick Williams, that is. The man who managed the Oakland Athletics to consecutive World Series championships in 1972 and 1973 was found outside his hotel room naked and masturbating. Williams was in town for the World Series of Fantasy Baseball Camp and could only dream that his public indecency conviction wasn't a reality. Williams pleaded no contest and was released after spending a night in jail. Williams was the only manager of three pennant-winning teams and title winners in four divisions.

CHAPTER 11

Tools of the Trade

BALLS, BATS AND HATS

They are the tools of the trade: helmets, gloves, shoes, caps, bats and balls. Yes, the ball—truly a fine object. Two pieces of white cowhide, stretched and stitched together 108 times. A sphere that brings delight and fear to fans and foes alike.

Most expensive ball

$3.2 million

The Six Million Dollar Man was a fictional TV character played by actor Lee Majors in the 1970s. But the $3.2-million ball is real. That's how much comic-book artist Todd McFarlane paid at auction for Mark McGwire's 70th home-run ball of the 1998 season.

Most expensive error ball

$93,500

If Bill Buckner could pay $93,500 to change history, he surely would. That's how much actor Charlie Sheen paid on August 4, 1992, for the ball hit by New York Met Mookie Wilson that went through the Boston Red Sox first baseman's legs in Game 6 of the 1986 World Series. The New York Mets tied the World Series on Buckner's error on October 25 and won the championship two nights later in Game 7. Sheen bought the ball at a New York City auction.

Least likely person to autograph baseballs in bulk

Mother Teresa

Forging a Joe DiMaggio or Mickey Mantle autograph is illegal. Forging Mother Teresa's is both illegal and sinful. Yet 26 people in California were indicted after the Federal Bureau of Investigations busted a sports memorabilia fraud ring in April 2000. "Operation Bullpen" found merchandise with the counterfeit autographs of DiMaggio, Mantle and Mother Teresa, the Catholic missionary and 1979 Nobel Peace Prize winner who died in 1997. Her falsified signature was found on dozens of baseballs seized by the police in the raid.

Only manager to invent a ball additive

"Lena" Blackburne, Chicago (AL)

Mud was Russell Aubrey "Lena" Blackburne's business. And his special Delaware River mud left its mark on baseball — and baseballs, thanks to American League umpires, who used it to remove a baseball's shine. Their National League cousins, however, didn't adopt the unlikely solvent league-wide until the 1950s. Blackburne, who took over from Ray Schalk as manager of the Chicago White Sox on July 4, 1928, managed the team through 1929 before quitting to market his mud.

Lowest price paid for a player in a trade

$100 and a bag of baseballs, March 28, 1983

Minor league prospect Keith Comstock changed organizations during spring training in 1983, but he didn't get a boost in self-esteem. The Oakland Athletics sold Comstock to the Detroit Tigers for $100 cash and a bag of baseballs. Time would show that Comstock was more valuable than that, however. The journeyman pitcher made his big league debut in 1984 with the Minnesota Twins, and continued his career until 1991 with the San Francisco Giants, San Diego Padres and Seattle Mariners.

Only player to use a vegetable in a game

Dave Bresnahan, Williamsport (class AA), August 28, 1987

Roger Bresnahan, baseball's first Hall of Fame catcher, introduced protective padding to the game. His great nephew, Dave, introduced the potato. The story goes that, during a class AA game against the Reading Phillies, the Cleveland Indians catching prospect went to the Williamsport Bills dugout to repair his glove. When Bresnahan returned behind home plate, he received the next pitch and threw what appeared to be a ball to third baseman Rob Swain, his roommate, who let Bresnahan's peeled potato fly past him into left field. Bresnahan then hid the real game ball and used it to tag the baserunner out at home. When the umpire realized the "tater trick" and reversed the call, manager Orlando Gomez pulled Bresnahan, and the Indians released him the next day for "jeopardizing the integrity of the game." But the Bills capitalized on the controversy the next day when they sold tickets for $1 to anyone with a potato. The guest of honor was Bresnahan himself, who paid his $50 fine to Gomez in spuds.

Most tampered balls a pitcher was found to possess in a game

3: Don Sutton, Los Angeles, July 14, 1978

At the plate, it's three strikes and you're out. On the pitching mound, it's three doctored balls and you're ejected. Los Angeles Dodgers pitcher Don Sutton learned that the hard way during a 1978 game, after umpire Doug Harvey found him with three balls that had been purposefully damaged to fool the batters. Sutton was bidding for his 200th career victory, but ended up a 4–1 loser to the St. Louis Cardinals after he was thrown out in the seventh inning.

First game using a yellow ball

St. Louis vs. Brooklyn, August 2, 1938

Why do balls have to be white? Brooklyn Dodgers general manager Larry MacPhail ventured to answer the age-old question, when he ordered the Dodgers to play yellow balls in a 6–2 win over the St. Louis Cardinals in the first half of an Ebbets Field doubleheader. Obviously, MacPhail's experiment never caught on, and today's balls remain white with red stitching.

First baseball equipment endorsed by a professional player

Louisville Slugger bat, 1905

Every athlete who endorses a product owes a small debt of gratitude to Honus Wagner, the pioneer of the practice. Wagner, who started his career in Louisville, Kentucky, got to know baseball bat manufacturer Bud Hillerich during his three seasons playing in the Derby state. Although he left to play for the Pittsburgh Pirates in 1900, Wagner kept in touch with Hillerich and would later sign a contract to endorse the innovator's Louisville Slugger bats.

First player to search bats for hits

Bill Caudill, Seattle, 1982

The Seattle Mariners had a mystery on their hands, and pitcher Bill Caudill wanted to crack the case. The Mariners were 2–7 early in 1982, so Caudill dressed up as Sherlock Holmes and used a magnifying glass to examine each and every bat to find out where the team's hitting power had gone. Caudill became somewhat of a folk hero in Seattle, where the Kingdome organist played "Theme from the Pink Panther" whenever he came into the game from the bullpen.

Most bats X-rayed

76: Sammy Sosa, 2003

Major League Baseball officials wondered exactly what was inside Sammy Sosa's bats, so they seized all 76 from his Wrigley Field locker and X-rayed them. Sosa had been ejected from a game and suspended for seven more when his bat shattered after he hit a first-inning ground ball on June 3, 2003. Umpires found pieces of cork amid the debris. Sosa claimed the bat was part of his batting practice stock and wasn't meant for use in the game. (Without Sosa, the Cubs won 3–2.) The rest of Sosa's bats tested negative for cork.

Most daring bat switch

Jason Grimsley, Cleveland, July 15, 1994

Cleveland Indians pitcher Jason Grimsley went to bat for team-mate Albert Belle during a 3–2 win over the Chicago White Sox in 1994, when umpire Dave Phillips seized Belle's bat on suspicion that it was corked. Phillips stored it in the umpires' locker room, but Grimsley found his way in there through a ceiling crawl space and replaced Belle's bat with another one like it. Phillips wasn't so easily fooled, however: the replacement bat had Paul Sorrento's name on it. Belle received a seven-game suspension.

Most unusual combustible bat substitute

Firework shaped like a torpedo

Honus Wagner celebrated the Fourth of July in style in 1909 when he came to bat without a bat. Instead, he used a torpedo-shaped firework that exploded when it came in contact with the first pitch the Pirates slugger faced. Pittsburgh still lost 4–2 to the Cincinnati Reds.

Most unusual non-combustible bat substitute

Table leg

It was two out in the bottom of the ninth, and Detroit Tigers first baseman Norm Cash knew he wouldn't spoil Nolan Ryan's second no-hitter of 1973 on July 15. Instead of a bat, he went to the plate with a table leg. The umpire ordered Cash to return with a real bat. He did, and popped out to shortstop Rudy Meoli to end the California Angels' 6–0 win over Detroit.

Biggest fine for throwing a splintered bat

$50,000: Roger Clemens, New York (AL), 2000

On July 8, 2000, New York Yankees pitcher Roger Clemens hit
New York Mets catcher Mike Piazza in the head with a pitch
during an interleague game at Yankee Stadium, giving Piazza a
concussion that kept him out of the All-Star game. The pair met
again during the second game of the World Series on October 22,
when Piazza hit a Clemens pitch foul. Piazza's bat disintegrated,
but Clemens picked up a piece and threw it at Piazza, who was
running for first because he thought the ball was fair. The benches
cleared and both teams came close to trading punches. The
episode of unsportsmanlike conduct cost Clemens $50,000.

Most days suspended for using a bat as a weapon

9: Juan Marichal, San Francisco, 1965

Had Juan Marichal used his bat as a weapon outside of Candlestick Park, he would have ended up in jail. Instead, the San
Francisco Giants pitcher escaped with a nine-day suspension and
$1,750 fine after attacking Los Angeles Dodgers catcher Johnny
Roseboro in the bottom of the third inning on August 22, 1965.
Marichal lost his temper after he claimed Roseboro nicked his ear
on throws to Dodgers pitcher Sandy Koufax, and whacked Roseboro, giving him a two-inch gash on the head. Members of both
teams restrained Marichal—still clutching the weapon—at first
base. Although the Giants were 4–3 winners, the Dodgers eventually won the pennant with a two-game lead over San Francisco.

Most obscene baseball card

Billy Ripken, Baltimore, 1989

In the Ripken family, Cal Ripken Jr.'s baseball cards are worth
more than brother Billy's—except perhaps one. In 1989, Billy
Ripken's Fleer baseball card shows him holding a bat with the

words "Fuck Face" in black ink on the butt of the bat. An unidentified teammate committed the prank, which didn't amuse Fleer when the company spotted the obscenity after the card hit the market. Corrections were made to later printings.

First game with batting helmets
April 20, 1941, Brooklyn vs. New York (NL)
They called it the Brooklyn Safety Cap, and it helped the Dodgers edge the New York Giants 10–9 at the Polo Grounds on April 20, 1941. The first big-league batting helmets were essentially protective plastic liners, invented by George Barnett and Walter Dandy of Johns Hopkins University.

First team to change hat color based on science
Cincinnati Reds, 1972
The Cincinnati Reds turned from gray to green in 1972 on the advice of an academic. The undersides of their caps were green until optics expert John Nash Ott said gray would have a positive effect on the players' mental health. It seemed to work. The Reds went from 79–83 in 1971 to 95–59 in 1972.

Most unusual headgear in a baseball card photograph
Umbrella hat
This Bud's for Jay. Chicago Cubs outfielder Jay Johnstone wore a Budweiser umbrella hat for his 1984 Topps baseball card, number 495 in the series.

Victim of worst preseason hat injury
Richie Sexson, Milwaukee, 2003
Richie Sexson found out too late that his cap was too small, as the Milwaukee Brewers first baseman readied for the Brewers' 2003 team photo shoot. The cap was size $6^5/_8$, one full size smaller than

his usual cap. Sexson strained his neck trying to get it to fit, and missed a spring training intrasquad game in Phoenix.

Best use of a teammate's shoes

Hank Aaron, Atlanta, 1973

During his pursuit of Babe Ruth's career home-run record, Hank Aaron didn't always wear his own shoes: he wore a pair that used to belong to Joe Pepitone. Pepitone, who played just three games for the Atlanta Braves in 1973 and went 4-for-11 with just one RBI before retiring, left two pairs of shoes behind when he departed during a road trip to St. Louis. Ralph Garr got one pair and Aaron, his outfield buddy, got the other.

Best aim with a glove

Fred Sanford, St. Louis (AL), 1947

St. Louis Browns pitcher Fred Sanford made a play for the ages in the first game of a doubleheader against the Red Sox at Fenway Park on July 27, 1947. Too bad the 4–3 Boston win wasn't televised. Boston's Jake Jones hit a foul ball with two out. Sanford feared it would be an infield hit, so he threw his mitt at the ball in an attempt to ensure it would be foul, but the glove caught the ball without Sanford's arm attached. Instead of ending the inning, Jones received an automatic triple because of a rule that forbids players from throwing equipment at a ball.

Biggest contract cancelled because of preseason equipment theft

$1 million: Ruben Rivera, New York (AL), March 12, 2002

Outfielder Ruben Rivera's career with the New York Yankees ended before it even had a chance to begin. Although it wasn't because of what he did on the field in spring training, but because of what he did in the locker room when no one was looking: he stole a bat and glove from Derek Jeter's locker and sold it for $2,500. Rivera later returned the items, but it was too late. The cousin of relief pitcher Mariano Rivera was released and his $1-million, one-year contract cancelled. Jeter normally sold game-used bats through a memorabilia company to raise money for his children's charity. But he didn't sell his gloves.

Most famous manicure claim by a pitcher
Joe Niekro, August 3, 1987
Nice nails, Niekro! Minnesota Twins pitcher Joe Niekro was facing the Angels in Anaheim in 1987, when home-plate umpire Tim Tschida got suspicious about his pitching technique. When the curious umpire reached the mound, an emery board fell from one of Niekro's pockets. Tschida decided the pitcher was using the board to scuff balls and ejected him in the fourth inning; he was then suspended for 10 days. (Niekro claimed he was using the board as a nail file.) Reliever Dan Schatzeder pitched the rest of the 11–3 win.

Biggest fine after suffering a self-inflicted laceration
$250: Rick Honeycutt, Seattle, 1980
Rick Honeycutt did a lousy job of concealing the thumbtack taped to his pitching glove at Seattle's Kingdome on September 30, 1980. After hitting a double, Kansas City Royal Willie Wilson told umpires that he saw a tack on the middle finger of the Mariner's glove. The umpires not only found the tack, but also noticed Honeycutt bleeding from the forehead. Honeycutt was ejected with two out, suspended 10 games and fined $250. Insult was added to injury when the Royals beat the Mariners 7–5 in 14 innings.

Shiniest earrings

Arthur Rhodes, Seattle, August 25, 2001

Seattle Mariners pitcher Arthur Rhodes wore flashy earrings during a 2001 game at Safeco Field. But they were too flashy for Cleveland Indians shortstop Omar Vizquel. When he came to bat in the ninth inning, he complained to the umpires that when the sun glanced off Rhodes's earrings, the shine was distracting and hurt his eyes. Third-base umpire Tim McClelland agreed, and ejected Rhodes. The Mariners beat the Indians 3–2 after another controversial Indians pitcher, John Rocker, committed a throwing error in the 11th inning.

Most expensive elbow chips

$23,600: Jeff Nelson, Seattle, 2002

You want a piece of me? You'll have to buy it! Seattle Mariners pitcher Jeff Nelson thought he was just doing a good deed for charity after surgery to remove bone chips from his right elbow on May 8, 2002. Nelson put the fragments up for auction on eBay, where the bidding reached $23,600, but the auction was halted 24 hours after it began. The website cited rules prohibiting the sale of human parts.

First major leaguer to play with an artificial hip

Bo Jackson, Chicago (AL), 1993

Being a Kansas City Royals outfielder and a Los Angeles Dodgers running back turned out to be too much for Bo Jackson's hip. His two-sport career almost ended in a 1991 National Football League playoff game against the Denver Broncos when he was forced to undergo hip replacement surgery. But he returned in 1993 with an artificial hip to lead the Chicago White Sox to the American League championship series.

Most bizarre warm-up injury

Vince Coleman, St. Louis, October 13, 1985

Hey, Vince, don't be a slow-poke. Get out of the way! Vince Cole-man's rookie season with the St. Louis Cardinals ended abruptly in bizarre fashion before the start of Game 4 of the 1985 National League championship series, when his left leg got tangled for less than a minute as the field tarp unrolled in Busch Stadium. Without him, the Cardinals beat the Los Angeles Dodgers 12–2 to tie the series at two games apiece. They advanced to the World Series but lost to the Kansas City Royals. The irony, of course, is that Coleman was known for his speed, having stolen 110 bases in his rookie season.

Least-popular musical instrument on a team bus

Harmonica: New York (AL), 1964

Yogi Berra wasn't fond of harmonica music, and especially after his team had just lost a game. The New York Yankees were smart-ing from a 5–0 loss—their fourth straight—to the Chicago White Sox on August 20, 1964, when infielder Phil Linz whipped out his harmonica in a bid to cheer up his teammates on the Yankees bus. But to the horror of manager Berra, Linz played "Mary Had a Little Lamb." Berra asked him to stop, as Mickey Mantle encour-aged him to play louder. Linz listened to Mantle, so Berra grabbed the instrument from Linz's hands in what has become known as "the Harmonica Incident."

Longest equipment supply relationship

100 seasons: Spalding balls

Albert Spalding pitched for Chicago in its National League debut on April 25, 1876, and managed the White Stockings to the first championship with a 52–14 record. But it was off-field in a factory where he made the biggest impact on the big leagues. In 1877, his A.G. Spalding and Brothers sporting goods company made a deal with the National League that for every Spalding ball used, he would pay $1 to the NL. Spalding died in 1915, but his company supplied balls to Major League Baseball until 1976—the NL's centennial year.

Most home runs in a season using a non-American bat
73: Barry Bonds, San Francisco, 2001
Barry Bonds become an American idol in 2001—with a little help from a piece of Canadian lumber. Bonds hit his 73rd home run on October 7 at Pacific Bell Park using a maple Rideau Crusher bat, manufactured by Ottawa's Sam Bat Company. (The Sam in Sam Bat is Sam Holman, a stage-hand at the National Arts Centre who succeeded in developing a bat stronger than traditional ash.)

Biggest fine for hitting a sausage
$2,432, Randall Simon, Pittsburgh, 2003
First baseman Randall Simon got himself in a real pickle during a game against the Brewers in Milwaukee on July 9, 2003. The Pittsburgh Pirate, wearing a mustard-yellow uniform, hit an Italian sausage mascot with his bat after the sixth inning at Milwaukee's Miller Field. Police managed to "ketchup" with Simon to fine him $432 for disorderly conduct. Major League Baseball spiced up the punishment with an additional $2,000 fine and a three-game suspension. (The sausage was actually 19-year-old Mandy Block, who was mildly shaken by the blow. Her Brewers co-workers— dressed as a bratwurst, a hot dog and a Polish sausage—were un- harmed.) Needless to say, Simon didn't relish the attention. He was originally arrested after the game for misdemeanor battery, but wasn't much of a hot dog at the plate. He grounded out as a pinch- hitter in the seventh inning of Milwaukee's 2–1, 12-inning win, and finished the season with the Chicago Cubs after a trade.

CHAPTER 12

All Dressed Up

UNIFORMS FOR SUCCESS

AND EXCESS

Look sharp and play sharp. Ballplayers can be very particular and peculiar about what they wear and how they wear it. For some, it's all about fashion. For others, it's just a matter of function. But do ballplayers and their teams dress for success or excess? Let history be the judge.

First retired jersey number

4: Lou Gehrig

When Lou Gehrig shocked America by retiring suddenly, the New York Yankees searched for ways to honor him. (The star first baseman was dying from amyotrophic lateral sclerosis, the debilitating disease that would eventually bear his name.) For starters, the Yankees decided to retire Gehrig's number four jersey at Yankee Stadium in an emotional ceremony on July 4, 1939. Jersey number retirement ceremonies are now common in all North American professional sports.

Only team to retire a jersey number before playing a game

Florida Marlins: 5

Florida's fish are fast. Before the Florida Marlins began their first National League game on April 5, 1993, they retired a jersey. Carl Barger, the team's late president, had died the previous December, and the Marlins honored him by retiring number five—the number worn by his favorite player, Joe DiMaggio. DiMaggio was at Joe Robbie Stadium to throw out the ceremonial opening pitch before the 6–3 Marlins win over the Los Angeles Dodgers.

Only team to honor a hockey player on its jersey

Montreal Expos, 2000

No matter how hard the Montreal Expos have tried, Montreal is still a hockey town. This was particularly obvious on June 1, 2000, when the Expos placed the number nine of hockey legend Maurice "Rocket" Richard on their jersey sleeves. The National Hockey League's first 50-goal scorer died May 27, 2000.

First numbered jerseys worn in a game

Cleveland Indians, 1929

You can always trust the New York Yankees to send the baseball world reeling—even during the off-season. On January 22, 1929, the Yankees announced their players would be the first to wear numbers on the backs of their jerseys. However, the April 16 opener at Yankee Stadium was rained out, so the Cleveland Indians were the first.

Only player to wear his hometown on his jersey

96: Bill Voiselle

Bill Voiselle was from Ninety-Six, South Carolina, and he wanted everyone to know. That's why he wore number 96 on the back of his uniform during his nine-year major league career with the New York Giants, Boston Braves and Chicago Cubs.

Only player with his birthdate on a jersey

17: Carlos May

There was never an excuse to miss Carlos May's birthday. May chose jersey number 17 with the Chicago White Sox in 1970, so the back of his jersey looked like a page from a calendar: May 17. That's also the date in 1948 that he was born in Birmingham, Alabama.

Biggest payment by a player for his jersey number

$25,000: Rickey Henderson, Toronto, 1993

Rickey Henderson felt naked without his favorite number, 24, on his jersey. So he paid Toronto Blue Jays teammate Turner Ward $25,000 for the digits on August 14, 1993, two weeks after Henderson was traded from the Oakland Athletics. Ward got a better deal than Oakland's Ron Hassey in 1989. Hassey gave up 24 to Henderson in exchange for a set of golf clubs, after Henderson returned to the A's following a stint with the New York Yankees.

Only player's jersey used to promote a TV station

Andy Messersmith, Atlanta, 1976

Atlanta Braves owner Ted Turner wanted to get the most out of his investment when he signed free-agent pitcher Andy Messersmith to a contract on April 10, 1976. Instead of putting Messersmith's name on his back, Turner put the word Channel to go with the number 17 in a ploy to hype his Atlanta TV station, WTBS. But National League officials forced Turner to put Messersmith's name back on the jersey.

Only number banned by an organization

13: Atlanta Braves

They can't avoid playing games on Friday the 13th, but the Atlanta Braves can afford to be superstitious in the jersey-numbering department. In 1978, the club banned the use of the number 13 on all jerseys, all the way down to their minor league affiliates. The ploy eventually paid off in 1980, when the Braves snapped a string of four last-place finishes in the National League's West Division.

Only fractional jersey number

$\frac{1}{8}$: Eddie Gaedel, 1951

A tiny player deserves a tiny number. And that's what Eddie Gaedel got when he made his only appearance for the St. Louis Browns on August 19, 1951. The three-foot-seven Gaedel walked while wearing jersey number ⅛.

Best jersey number for home runs

44

If you want to be a big-league slugger, hand-eye coordination and big muscles will only get you so far. What you really need is to wear number 44, just like three of the top-12 sluggers on the career home-run list. Hank Aaron, the all-time major league leader, had 755. Reggie Jackson, number eight on the list, had 563. Willie McCovey, who is tied with Ted Williams at 12th place, hit 521. Combined, the three men hit 1,839 homers.

Only jersey retired while a player was on another team's active roster

3: *Harold Baines*

They love Harold Baines in Chicago. In fact, the White Sox retired his number three jersey after he was traded to the Texas Rangers in 1989, then un-retired it when he returned to play in 1996 and 2000. The outfielder and designated hitter retired in 2001 after 22 years in the American League.

Greatest player whose uniform number has not been retired

Ty Cobb

Ty Cobb recorded a lot of superlative numbers at the plate and on the diamond, but his jersey number is recorded nowhere. That's because he played with the Detroit Tigers and Philadelphia Athletics before jersey numbers were standard.

Least successful dress-down protest

Dan Friend, Chicago (NL), August 30, 1897

Dan Friend made some enemies with umpires when he was substituted into an 1897 game. Friend, a pitcher, replaced Chicago White Stocking Cap Anson in left field after Anson was ejected for arguing a strike call, but took the field wearing a bathrobe and ball cap. The New York Giants protested and Friend was ordered to change into proper attire. That was the only decision that went the Giants' way, however: the White Stockings were 7–5 winners.

Least successful major league uniform experiment
Color-coded jerseys, 1882
Fans at National League ballparks in 1882 must have felt like they were at the racetrack, with players looking like jockeys in colored uniforms that corresponded with their field positions. All pants, belts and ties remained white, but pitchers wore light blue jerseys and pants while catchers sported scarlet. First basemen were decked out in scarlet and white; second basemen wore orange and black, and third basemen gray and white. In the outfield, leftfielders wore white; centerfielders, red and black, and right fielders, gray. The first substitute was in green; the second wore brown. But by 1883, teams were back to the traditional home whites and road grays.

First player to credit a teammate's pants for a grand slam
Carlos Pena, Detroit Tigers, May 19, 2003
Carlos Pena's pants seemed a tad small on May 19, 2003. So he asked teammates before the game if he could borrow a bigger pair. Dmitri Young volunteered his, and Pena proceeded to hit three home runs — including a grand slam — while recording seven RBIs for the Detroit Tigers against the Cleveland Indians. Although the Tigers lost 10–9, Pena told everyone who would listen that it was Young's pants that had given him extra power at the plate. Obviously, Young wanted his pants back.

Least-popular team uniform experiment
Bermuda shorts, Chicago White Sox, 1976
Chicago White Sox owner Bill Veeck was long on ideas, short on

imagination, when he outfitted his team with Bermuda shorts for a doubleheader on August 8, 1976. Even 67-year-old manager Paul Richards had to expose his knobby knees. To avoid injury while stealing bases (amazingly, five White Sox did so), the players wore foam rubber pads in their long socks, but the White Sox still beat the pants off the Kansas City Royals 5–2 in the opener. The players reverted to traditional wear for the second game, which didn't make Veeck happy, especially when the team lost 7–1 to the Royals. (The White Sox weren't the first professional baseball team to wear shorts. On April 1, 1950, the Pacific Coast League's Hollywood Stars wore T-shirts and striped shorts during a game with the Portland Beavers.)

Most times a hat fell off a pitcher in a World Series game

37: Jim Bouton, New York (AL), October 10, 1964
New York Yankees fans didn't care whether or not Jim Bouton could keep his hat on when he pitched against the St. Louis Cardinals in Game 3 of the 1964 World Series. Bouton lost his lid 37 times during his 2–1, complete-game victory.

Biggest jersey number differential

99: 2003
The St. Louis Cardinals couldn't go any higher, so they went as low as they could when leftfielder So Taguchi, who wore number 99, was replaced by pinch-hitter (number 0) Kerry Robinson during an 8–5 loss to the Cincinnati Reds on August 29, 2003.

Worst jersey spelling error

Angees, 2003
Adam Riggs thought he was playing left field for the Anaheim Angels on August 17, 2003. Turns out, he was starting for the "Angees." The manufacturer of the defending World Series

champions' jerseys misspelled the word "Angels" on the front of Riggs's jersey, but nobody noticed until after he took his spot on the field in the first inning of a game against the Detroit Tigers. The Angels beat the Tigers 11–7, and Riggs's jersey was sent back to the factory, where workers were reminded how to spell A-N-G-E-L-S.

Number of letters in the longest full name of a major league player

45: Alan Mitchell Edward George Patrick Henry Gallagher
Just call him Al. Alan Mitchell Edward George Patrick Henry Gallagher was a third baseman for the San Francisco Giants and California Angels from 1970 to 1973. Mitchell had five middle names, but only his surname—Gallagher—appeared on the back of his jersey.

CHAPTER 13

Fan Frenzy

PEOPLE POWER

Decade by decade, the stadiums get bigger and brighter, the ballplayers get paid more and the price of a ticket rises. But the fans are always there, renewing their devotion to the game they love. Sometimes they express it in quantity or quality; other times, they find clever and odd ways to show their appreciation.

Biggest crowd at a major league game

93,103: Los Angeles, May 7, 1959

Before the Los Angeles Dodgers had Dodger Stadium, they played from 1958 to 1961 at Los Angeles Memorial Coliseum. The cavernous site of the 1932 and 1984 Summer Olympics hosted the largest crowd to see a baseball game in the United States: a 6–2 exhibition win by the New York Yankees. The 1959 game was a benefit to honor paralyzed Dodgers catcher Roy Campanella, who almost died from a career-ending car crash on January 28, 1958.

Biggest single season attendance

4,483,350: Colorado, 1993

There are 4.3 million people in Colorado, but the state's major league team, the Colorado Rockies, counted 4,483,350 turnstile clicks during their inaugural season at Mile High Stadium in Denver.

Biggest intentionally fraudulent attendance

58,667: Portland, Oregon, July 18, 2002

The Portland Beavers' bean counters were having a bushel of fun when they claimed 58,667 people saw a 9–1 loss to the visiting Edmonton Trappers. In fact, there were only 12,969 fans at PGE Park for the Pacific Coast League game on Arthur Andersen Appreciation Night. The class AAA Beavers were poking fun at Texas power company Enron's beleaguered accounting firm when they allowed anyone named Arthur or Andersen in free and invited fans to bring paper for shredding at the ballpark. (Arthur Andersen executives had admitted to shredding important documents to hide Enron's financial woes; in 2001, the company filed one of the biggest bankruptcies in history.) But the Beavers had financial problems of their own, losing $8 million in their first season after moving from Albuquerque, New Mexico. Ironically, their ballpark was sponsored by Portland General Electric, an Enron subsidiary.

Smallest crowd for a major league game

12: Troy, New Jersey, September 27, 1881

Blame it on the rain. Only a dozen fans came to see the visiting Chicago White Stockings beat the Troy Trojans 10–8 in a National League game played during a downpour in 1881.

Smallest crowd in professional baseball

0: Charleston, South Carolina, July 8, 2002

The record set by the Charleston RiverDogs in 2002 can only be tied. When the Columbia Red Stixx came to play the class A South Atlantic League game, the RiverDogs held Nobody Night. Not until the game—and attendance— were deemed official after five innings were fans allowed into the ballpark. In keeping with the night's theme, the ceremonial first pitch was thrown from outside the park. The stunt got worldwide attention, but it didn't get the RiverDogs a win. They lost 4–2.

Most rabbits feet distributed at a major league ballpark

15,000: Cleveland, July 14, 1951

There were a lot of rabbits hobbling about on stumps after the Cleveland Indians gave away thousands of rabbits feet to fans on Beat Eddie Lopat Night in 1951. The Tribe was hoping to prevent New York Yankees pitcher Lopat from getting his 12th consecutive win against the club. Fans attending Municipal Stadium received the good luck charms, but one fan brought a black cat that he tossed at Lopat. The hex worked: Lopat lost 8–2. He retired four years later as a Baltimore Oriole with a career record of 40 wins and 12 losses in meetings with the Indians.

Most short-order cooks admitted free to a ball game

1,323: *San Diego, June 28, 1974*

Houston Astros third baseman Doug Rader donned a chef's hat and apron and served his team's starting menu, er lineup, to the umpires in a frying pan. But the host San Diego Padres had the recipe for victory on Short-Order Cooks Night, and Rader was the first ingredient in the unusual promotion. After Padres owner Ray Kroc used the public address system during the team's 1974 home opener, Rader quipped that Kroc—chairman of the McDonald's fast food restaurant chain—"must think he's dealing with a bunch of short-order cooks." The Padres then allowed 1,323 genuine short-order cooks into Jack Murphy Stadium free for the 5–4 win. Rader's performance at the plate was anything but tasty, however. He went 1-for-5 with an error and committed the final out of the game on a bases-loaded fly ball.

Most fans admitted to a game for free with freshly shaved heads

512: *Seattle, May 19, 1994*

Give us your hair and we'll give you a ticket. A total of 512 Seattle Mariner fans took advantage of the free head shaves and became bald on Jay Buhner Haircut Night to honor the popular, hairless outfielder. Not only were heads glistening, but faces were smiling as Buhner scored the 5–4 winning run against the Texas Rangers at Seattle's Kingdome in the bottom of the ninth inning.

Age of youngest fan to affect the outcome of a game

12: *Jeffrey Maier, New York*

The kid did it! Baltimore Orioles rightfielder Tony Tarasco caught Derek Jeter's blast at the wall in the first game of 1996's American League championship series. But the ball disappeared from his glove into the hands of 12-year-old New York Yankees fan Jeffrey

Maier, who plucked the ball from Tarasco. Umpire Rich Garcia ruled it a home run and the game was tied. The Yankees began the series with a 5–4 win and advanced to the World Series in six games.

Longest entertaining game delay

70 minutes: Montreal, June 6, 1978

Long before Montreal gave the world Cirque du Soleil, the Montreal Expos and visiting San Diego Padres put on a show under the big top at Olympic Stadium. The Expos were leading the Padres 2–0 when the lights went off with one out in the bottom of the sixth. Derrel Thomas of the Padres didn't want to wait for the game to resume to have fun, however: he tried throwing a ball through the giant hole in the unfinished building's roof. He then tried rolling balls down the third-base line to home plate while Padres rookie shortstop Ozzie Smith performed back flips and cartwheels and Expo Warren Cromartie fell flat on his face in jest. The circus-like atmosphere ended when the game was suspended after 70 minutes of dead time. Montreal scored another two runs for the 4–0 win when the game continued on June 7.

Only Rookie of the Year who opened beer bottles with an eye socket

"Super" Joe Charbonneau, 1980

"Super" Joe Charbonneau was a folk hero to many Cleveland Indians fans, who believed he was the savior who would lead the Indians back to the Promised Land: the World Series. And how could you doubt Charbonneau's extraordinary talents? He could open beer bottles with one of his eye sockets and drink beer through his nose with a straw. But although his 23-home-run debut in 1980 earned him Rookie of the Year honors, Charbonneau was out of major league ball two years later.

First player to prevent an on-field flag-burning
Rick Monday, April 25, 1976
Chicago Cub Rick Monday saved the Stars and Stripes from being torched in Dodger Stadium's outfield during the bottom of the fourth inning of a 1976 game, when a man and a youth ran on-field and poured an accelerant on the Star-Spangled Banner they were carrying. Monday grabbed the flag, while security guards pounced on the pair. His gesture earned the applause of Dodger fans, who were just as happy to see their team win the game 5–4.

Only team to employ a good luck monkey
Anaheim Angels
Anaheim Angels fans went bananas because of a monkey on June 6, 2000. The Halos were losing an interleague game to the San Francisco Giants at home when the operator of Edison Field's video scoreboard flashed a clip from the movie *Ace Ventura: Pet Detective* showing a bouncing capuchin monkey. The Angels turned a 3–0 deficit into a 6–5 win after the primate's debut. Thereafter, whenever the Angels needed a lift, they played the monkey clip. The so-called "Rally Monkey" also played a big role in turning up the volume of the cheering fans during the team's 2002 World Series championship drive. It just so happened that the Angels also beat the Giants in the Fall Classic for their first title.

First player charged for killing a seagull
Dave Winfield, New York (AL), August 4, 1983
New York Yankee Dave Winfield silenced two birds at Toronto's Exhibition Stadium in August 1983, when he beat the Blue Jays with a home run and game-winning RBI—and killed a seagull. Winfield threw the ball that hit the bird just before the Jays batted in the third inning. A ball boy ran onto the field and covered the motionless bird with a towel, and Toronto police booked Winfield

on animal cruelty charges. Released on $500 bail, Winfield was ordered to return for an August 12 court date, but the prosecutor angered Blue Jays fans and animal lovers alike by ruling the death accidental and dropping the charges.

Best prize for a New York Mets Most Valuable Player
Amphicar, September 15, 1963
Ron Hunt got the best of both worlds when New York Mets fans voted him Most Valuable Player in 1963, an honor that came with an Amphicar (an automobile that doubles as a boat). Hunt's was one of only 3,878 Amphicars built by the German company of the same name. The amphibious car was capable of traveling at seven miles per hour in water and 70 miles per hour on land.

Most expensive baseball card
$1.1 million: Honus Wagner, 1909 American Tobacco series
When he played for the Pittsburgh Pirates a century ago, Honus Wagner was not a million-dollar ballplayer—but he is now. In fact, the Hall of Fame shortstop's face is on the most valuable baseball card of them all, one that sold on eBay in 2000 for $1.1 million. The reason the Wagner card is worth so much is that it's one of only a few ever produced. Wagner never liked the idea of being on a baseball card as part of a promotion to sell cigarettes.

Most money given to a fan after a player hit for the cycle
$1 million
Pamela Altazan has a million reasons to be Alex Rodriguez's biggest fan. On June 5, 1997, Altazan was chosen in a draw to win $1 million if the Seattle Mariner, nicknamed "A-Rod," singled, doubled, tripled and homered in the 14–6 win over Detroit at Tiger Stadium. He did, and she won.

Most expensive chewing gum used by a player

$10,000: Luis Gonzalez

The owner of a Wisconsin-based medical supplies company got in a sticky situation on April 15, 2002—voluntarily, when he paid $10,000 in a fundraising auction for Bazooka gum chewed by Arizona Diamondbacks star Luis Gonzalez to benefit a Minnesota school's scholarship fund. The auction started with a different piece of gum, however, one salvaged after a March 7 spring training game in Tucson, Arizona, by a Minnesota sports collectibles dealer. Bidding reached $3,275 before the auction was halted due to speculation that the gum hadn't been chewed by Gonzalez after all. To avoid any more problems, Gonzalez chewed another piece of gum in front of the TV cameras, then placed it in a small, transparent box.

Most expensive tickets to the shortest exhibition of play

$2.50 and $1

The prices were so low that scalpers could afford to take the day off, but 1,200 fans barely got their money's worth. After paying $2.50 for grandstand tickets and $1 for bleacher seats at Yankee Stadium on August 18, 1983, all ticket-holders got was nine minutes and 41 seconds of play. (The Yankees had tried charging regular admission prices for the game, but two fan-led court injunctions forced the discounts.) Kansas City Royal Hal McRae struck out in the ninth and New York went down in order to ratify the 5–4 Yankees win. The score was the same when the regular-season game ended in controversy on July 24, after Royal George

Brett's two-out, two-run homer in the ninth was disallowed because his bat surface contained too much pine tar. Major League Baseball ordered the teams to replay the last 1⅓ innings.

Lowest modern-day price for beer in a big-league park
10 cents

These days, a dime won't even buy a sip of beer at a big-league ballpark. But in Cleveland on June 4, 1974, suds were 10 cents a cup—while supplies lasted. Hooligans, however, were a dime a dozen during the game between the Indians and Texas Rangers at Municipal Stadium. The teams were tied in the ninth inning and the home team had two men on base with two out when a riot erupted. Umpire Nestor Chylak awarded a 9–0 win to the visiting Rangers after Indians officials failed to control the hopped-up crowd.

Most scrap metal required for free tickets
10 pounds

If you were a kid with 10 pounds of scrap metal, you were welcomed to the Polo Grounds for free on September 26, 1942, when the material was gathered and donated to the war effort for use in building weapons and supplies. The Giants took the first game of the doubleheader 6–4 over the Boston Braves. They also led 5–2 in the second game, which was later forfeited to the Braves when youngsters swarmed the field.

Worst celebrity anthem singer
Roseanne Barr

They forgot to play the laugh track when sitcom star Roseanne Barr sang the "Star Spangled Banner" before a San Diego Padres game on July 25, 1990. After screaming the lyrics into a microphone near home plate, she tried to act like a ballplayer by scratching her crotch and spitting at the dirt. She was not invited for an encore performance. Padres players apologized to the disgusted fans the only way they knew how: by beating the Cincinnati Reds 10–4.

Only game interrupted by a busker

Cincinnati vs. New York (NL), April 20, 2001

Times Square's most-famous, least-dressed busker followed the New York Mets to Cincinnati in April 2001 — right onto the field during the second inning. But this wasn't just any old busker. It was Robert John Burck II, better known as the "Naked Cowboy," who invited himself onto the diamond wearing only his trademark cowboy hat, cowboy boots and briefs. But instead of the guitar he plays for tourists in the Big Apple, Burck came equipped with a glove. Police removed the former Cincinnati resident from the field and the game resumed, with the Reds eventually winning 9–5.

Only known Yankees fan to have her rear end signed by the team

"Jane Doe"

Only the woman who collected the autographs of the 1979 New York Yankees on her buns knows who she is, so we'll just call her Jane Doe — the 20-year-old blonde who hopped aboard the Yankees team bus after a 9–1 win over the Chicago White Sox at Comiskey Park on August 1, 1979. Onboard, she dropped her pants and asked the players to sign her rear. They gleefully obliged. Manager Billy Martin even snapped some photographs.

Only president stopped from jumping onto the field by the Secret Service

President Dwight Eisenhower, April 13, 1954

Ike was giddy about Mickey. After a two-run homer by the Washington Senator to beat the New York Yankees 5–3 in the

10th inning, President Dwight Eisenhower jumped out of his seat and headed for the field. Eisenhower wanted to congratulate Vernon, his favorite player. Secret Service agents, however, halted the commander-in-chief and brought Vernon to the president's box instead. On May 27, Eisenhower gave Vernon a silver bat for winning the 1953 batting title.

Most incumbent presidents from two countries at a major league game

2: President George H.W. Bush and Hosni Mubarak, April 3, 1989
It was an Opening Day doubleheader of a different kind. Instead of two games on April 3, 1989, Baltimore Orioles fans got a visit from two presidents from different countries at Oriole Park, when President George H.W. Bush and Egyptian president Hosni Mubarak watched five innings of the Orioles' 5–4 win over the Boston Red Sox. Mubarak's visit to an American baseball game came a century after the Chicago White Stockings and a National League All-Star team visited Cairo, Egypt, on a 50-game world tour.

Only game outside Washington attended by the U.S. president and vice-president
California vs. Baltimore, September 6, 1995
Because of national security, rarely do the president and vice-president appear in public at the same venue. But baseball history took precedence the day Cal Ripken Jr. played his 2,131st consecutive game to surpass Lou Gehrig's iron-man record. President Bill Clinton and Vice-President Al Gore made the short trip from Washington, D.C., to witness Ripken's milestone and the 8–0 Baltimore Orioles win over the California Angels.

Only ballplayer shot by a Lithuanian-speaking stalker

Eddie Waitkus, Philadelphia, 1949

Ruth Ann Steinhagen was a typist so obsessed with Eddie Waitkus that she spent her spare time learning to speak Lithuanian—Waitkus's first language. After a game on June 14, 1949, Waitkus returned to his Chicago hotel to a message asking him to go to room 1297A. Steinhagen answered the door and shot the Phillies player. Waitkus missed the rest of the season, but was named Comeback Player of the Year in 1950. Steinhagen's stalking stunt earned her three years in a mental hospital.

Strangest ballplayer kidnapping story

Charles "Flint" Rhem, September 19, 1930

Rum at the barrel of a gun belonging to gangster scum. That's the short version of why St. Louis Cardinals pitcher Charles "Flint" Rhem—scheduled to pitch against the Brooklyn Dodgers in September 1930—went missing for more than two days. When he resurfaced, Rhem claimed gangsters had kidnapped him, then held him at gunpoint and forced him to drink rum.

Biggest explosive thrown at autograph-seeking fans

M-100: Vince Coleman, New York (NL), July 24, 1993

Some ballplayers shun autograph seekers. But Vince Coleman almost blew them up in 1993, by throwing a firecracker at a group of fans waiting outside Dodger Stadium. The player was riding with New York Mets teammate Bobby Bonilla in a Jeep belonging to Los Angeles Dodger Eric Davis, when he threw an M-100—the equivalent of a third of a stick of dynamite—out the window. An 11-year-old boy and 2½-year-old girl were injured in the blast, and Coleman was convicted of misdemeanor possession of an explosive. The Mets released Coleman, despite his apology.

It wasn't the first such explosive incident of the season, either: on July 7, Mets pitcher Bret Saberhagen threw firecrackers at a pack of reporters.

Earliest non-holiday use of fireworks to repel insects
Baltimore vs. Chicago (AL), June 2, 1959

The Fourth of July was more than a month away when fireworks were used during a Baltimore Orioles game against the host Chicago White Sox—not in celebration of a home run, however, but in desperation. Groundskeepers were trying to get rid of the thousands of gnats that had invaded the ballpark, and caused a 28-minute delay by smoking out the critters. The Orioles beat the White Sox 3–2.

Longest game-delaying brawl not seen by fans
5 minutes: Pittsburgh vs. Los Angeles, August 25, 1981

There was no punch-by-punch play-by-play when the Los Angeles Dodgers and Pittsburgh Pirates brawled in the bowels of Three Rivers Stadium in April 1981. During their sixth inning at-bats, Pirates pitcher Pascual Perez clipped Dodgers Bill Russell and Dusty Baker on the hand before umpire Dutch Rennert warned Perez and the Pirates' manager, Tanner. When the inning ended, Perez challenged Dodger Reggie Smith to a fight under the grandstand—emptying the dugouts as the four-man umpiring crew ran to the scene of the five-minute mêlée. The teams eventually returned to the field, and the Pirates rallied with four runs in the ninth but lost 9–7 in the 11th inning.

First and last major league anti-disco music rally
Comiskey Park, Chicago, July 12, 1979

The biggest failure of all of Bill Veeck's innovative promotions wasn't his own idea. His son, Mike, suggested Disco Demolition

Night: every fan that brought a disco album got into Comiskey Park for 98 cents. The albums were then collected and destroyed between games when the Chicago White Sox hosted a double-header with the Detroit Tigers. At least, that's what was supposed to happen. But no one expected 5,000 fans to jump on-field after the pile of records was exploded with dynamite. Umpire Dave Phillips was not amused. The field was missing chunks of sod and was littered with broken vinyl, and he postponed the game. American League president Lee MacPhail later awarded the Tigers a 9–0 forfeit win.

Quietest ballgames

Jersey City, New Jersey, April 18, 1909
Charleston, South Carolina, July 14, 2003

Shhhh! We're trying to tie a record! When the Charleston RiverDogs hosted Silent Night in 2003 for a game with the Capital City Bombers, librarians replaced Riley Park's ushers, golf marshals waved "Quiet, Please" signs atop the dugouts and a tennis umpire was seated behind home plate. Sign language was used instead of a public address announcer and national anthem singer. And just in case the 2,924 fans still needed help keeping mum, they all received pieces of duct tape to cover their mouths. The home team quietly won 4–2 in its headline-grabbing attempt to meet the 94-year-old record for quietest game. (Jersey City management had asked fans to keep quiet on April 18, 1909, for a game against the New York Highlanders. They were flouting civic laws prohibiting Sunday baseball.)

Most expensive convicted player available for rent to fans

$3,500: Jose Canseco

For $2,500 through his personal website, retired journeyman slugger Jose Canseco offered fans the chance to hang out with him for an afternoon at his home in South Florida. A limousine ride from the airport was included, but travel and accommodations were not, though for an extra $1,000, you could spend a whole day with Jose. Canseco, who was sentenced to two years' house arrest in March 2003 on an aggravated battery conviction and later jailed for violating his probation by testing positive for steroids, was trying to raise funds to cover his legal bills.

Fan most blamed for home team's playoff demise

Steve Bartman, Chicago, October 14, 2003

Everyone wants a souvenir, and baseball fan Steve Bartman was no different. But he never imagined so many Chicago Cubs fans would scorn him after the game at Wrigley Field on October 14, 2003. The Cubs were leading the Florida Marlins 3–0 with one out in the eighth inning—five outs from winning the National League championship and advancing to their first World Series since 1945. Bartman reached for a foul ball, unaware that left-fielder Moises Alou was jockeying to catch it. The Marlins subsequently rallied to win 8–3, and Bartman, who failed to catch the ball, was escorted from the stadium by security guards for his own safety. The Marlins won Game 7 a night later to earn a trip to the World Series. Almost two months later, the infamous ball was auctioned off to a Chicago restaurant for $106,600.

CHAPTER 14

A League of Their Own

THE LORDS OF THE DIAMOND

They're the ones who pay the players to play the tunes, the ones whose investments can mean harmony in the ballpark or pure pandemonium. Some are in it just for the money, others just for fun. They're the owners. And without them, we'd have a game or a sport, but not an industry.

Most butterflies owned by a major league team owner

850,000: Arthur C. Allyn Jr., Chicago (AL)

Arthur Allyn never collected a pennant while he owned the Chicago White Sox from 1961 to 1969, he was too busy amassing one of the world's biggest butterfly collections. In 1981, Allyn's $2.4-million collection of 850,000 specimens was donated to the University of Florida, where the winged creatures were put on display at the Allyn Museum of Entomology at the Sarasota Jungle Gardens.

First owner to order the arrest of a streaker via a public address system

Ray Kroc, April 9, 1974, San Diego

Ray Kroc couldn't stay silent while his San Diego Padres were losing their 1974 home opener at Jack Murphy Stadium against the Houston Astros on April 9, 1974. In the eighth inning, he grabbed the public address announcer's microphone to apologize for his team's play. But a male streaker ran across the field during his impromptu speech. "Get that streaker off the field, throw him in jail!" Kroc bellowed into the microphone.

Cheapest owner of a major league team and fast food chain

Ray Kroc, San Diego Padres and McDonald's

San Diego Padres owner Ray Kroc wanted some company at Wrigley Field when he went to see his San Diego Padres play the Chicago Cubs. Problem was, he wasn't willing to pay for it. Kroc was in Chicago to meet McDonald's franchisees, but they had to buy their own tickets to the game on June 17, 1974. The notoriously frugal Kroc explained that the Padres needed the 27-cent-per-ticket visitors' share of the gate receipts. But those franchise owners who did pay up got their money's worth. San Diego beat the Cubs 7–5 in 13 innings.

First Mexican-American owner of a major league team

Arte Moreno, Anaheim

Viva los Angels! On May 22, 2003, when Arte Moreno bought the
defending World Series champion Anaheim Angels from Walt
Disney Co. for $184 million, he gave manager Mike Scioscia and
general manager Bill Stoneman red sombreros to celebrate.
Moreno, a Tucson, Arizona-native and baseball's first Mexican-
American owner, made his millions in outdoor advertising.

Fewest baseball games attended by a team owner

o: Hiroshi Yamauchi, Seattle

Hiroshi Yamauchi had never seen his Seattle Mariners
play. For that matter, the billionaire chairman of the Nin-
tendo video games company had never been to a major
league game, period. And when he finally did get tickets to
his first ballgame (at the Tokyo Dome, where the Mariners
and Oakland Athletics were to open the 2003 season with
a pair of games on March 25 and 26), the games were
cancelled due to the fears of terrorist attacks against any
Americans abroad during the American-led invasion of Iraq.

Biggest fine for being a Nazi-sympathizing owner

$25,000: Marge Schott, Cincinnati

Cincinnati Reds owner Marge Schott had a lot to answer for
during 1992's off-season. Reporters revealed that she owned a
Nazi armband, respected Adolf Hitler and frequently made
racist comments. Schott was fined $25,000 by Major League
Baseball on February 3, 1993, and banned from running the
Reds for a year.

Longest strike in major league history

234 days: August 12, 1994 to April 2, 1995

The Seattle Mariners beat the Oakland Athletics 8–1 in what turned out to be the last major league game of the 1994 season on August 12. Because on September 14, the rest of the season — including the World Series — was cancelled. The strike by the Major League Baseball Players Association continued until April 2, 1995, when owners and players agreed to a new contract. Action resumed April 25, when the Los Angeles Dodgers edged the Florida Marlins 8–7 in Miami. Like all MLBPA job action, the strike's central issue was player salaries.

First commissioner of baseball

Judge Kenesaw Mountain Landis, November 12, 1920

The title sounds important, but the commissioner is really the executive director and spokesman for the owners committee. The first man to hold the job was Kenesaw Mountain Landis, a judge who was best known for fining Standard Oil $29 million in an antitrust lawsuit that was later overturned by a higher court. The owners charged Landis with the task of cleaning up the game's tarnished image in the wake of the scandalous 1919 World Series, in which eight Chicago White Sox players were implicated in a gambling affair.

First Olympian to serve as baseball commissioner

Peter Ueberroth

Peter Ueberroth went from organizing the greatest sports spectacle on earth to overseeing the greatest sport in America. Ueberroth was head of the Los Angeles Olympic Organizing Committee for the 1984 Summer Games, then succeeded baseball's Bowie Kuhn in the commissioner's office on October 1, 1984. Ueberroth resigned before the 1989 season, and mounted an unsuccessful bid to purchase the California Angels in 1995.

Most-suspended franchise owner

George Steinbrenner, New York (AL)

George Steinbrenner made his millions in shipping. But no matter how hard they tried, Major League Baseball officials couldn't convince the controversial New York Yankees owner to sail off into the horizon. Cleveland-native Steinbrenner and his business partners purchased the Bronx-based team in 1973 for $10 million from CBS. Just a year later, Steinbrenner was found guilty of making illegal donations to Richard Nixon's Republican presidential campaign. Commissioner Bowie Kuhn banned Steinbrenner from the game for two years, but allowed him back 15 months later (President Ronald Reagan pardoned Steinbrenner in January 1989). Steinbrenner was banned again in 1990, for three years, when Commissioner Fay Vincent found he gave a man $40,000 to uncover unflattering information about Yankee Dave Winfield; Steinbrenner was desperate to avoid paying bonus money to the outfielder's charity.

Most money invested in a major league team by a crooner

$250,000: Bing Crosby, 1947

When Bing Crosby bought a 15 per cent stake in the Pittsburgh Pirates for $250,000 in 1947, in a group led by John Galbreath, he wasn't dreaming of a white Christmas. He was dreaming of a World Series. After Pittsburgh traded for Hank Greenberg and signed him to baseball's first $100,000 contract in 1947, Crosby celebrated by recording "Goodbye Mr. Ball, Goodbye" with Greenberg and Groucho Marx. Greenberg later invested in the Cleveland Indians, who were minority-owned by Crosby's showbiz buddy Bob Hope.

Most senior baseball executive fired for racist comments

Al Campanis, Los Angeles, April 8, 1987

Los Angeles Dodgers owner Peter O'Malley made baseball history when he fired general manager Al Campanis for the racist comments he made on ABC's *Nightline* with Ted Koppel on April 6, 1987. Campanis, on the show to discuss the 40th anniversary of Jackie Robinson's major league debut with the Dodgers when they were based in Brooklyn, claimed African-Americans lacked the skills to be field managers or general managers. Campanis had the skills to play just seven games for the 1943 Dodgers, but remained with the organization until two days after his *Nightline* appearance.

Most money offered by an owner for growing facial hair

$300: Charlie Finley, Oakland, 1972

Oakland Athletics owner Charlie Finley wanted to turn baseball upside down. Whereas most teams had anti-facial-hair policies, Finley actively encouraged players to keep the razor at bay. In 1972, he inserted a clause into every player's contract offering a $300 bonus per moustache, and facial hair fever swept the A's. Oakland—dubbed the "Moustache Gang"—won the first of three consecutive World Series. The most famous moustache on the roster belonged to pitcher Rollie Fingers, who fashioned his handlebar style.

Biggest cost-cutting measure by a World Series-winning owner

Wayne Huizenga, Florida, 1998

As quickly as Wayne Huizenga bought a World Series, he held a fire sale. The Florida Marlins owner signed $89 million worth of free agents to contracts after 1996 to turn his expansion team into a contender. Pitcher Alex Fernandez, leftfielder Moises Alou and third baseman Bobby Bonilla helped the Marlins finish 92–70 to become the first wildcard team to win the World Series. Huizenga, a waste disposal and video-rental tycoon, wouldn't tolerate a $30 million loss, however, and wanted to sell the franchise. But as he looked for buyers, the team's financial woes were temporarily solved by the departure of Alou and star pitchers Kevin Brown, Dennis Cook, Al Leiter and Robb Nen. The Marlins then traded Bonilla, rightfielder Gary Sheffield, catcher Charles Johnson and outfielder Jim Eisenreich to the Los Angeles Dodgers for Mike Piazza and Todd Zeile on May 15, 1998 (Piazza was dealt to the New York Mets a week later). With no chance of defending the title, however, the Marlins went 54–108 in 1998 — 52 games out of first place. By season's end, shortstop Edgar Renteria and outfielder Craig Counsell were the only regular Marlins remaining.

Most hated owner
Harry Frazee, Boston Red Sox
Boston Red Sox fans will never forgive owner Harry Frazee for selling Babe Ruth to the New York Yankees. Frazee was so hated in Beantown that a cab driver once punched him in the mouth. The Broadway show producer bought the Red Sox after the team won its third World Series in 1916; his team won another championship in 1918. But with attendance down at the ballpark and on Broadway during World War I, Frazee needed cash, and his biggest baseball assets were Babe Ruth and Fenway Park. So on December 26, 1919, he sold Ruth to Col. Jacob Ruppert and the New York Yankees for $125,000 and a $300,000 loan, with Fenway as collateral. Ruth then led the Yankees to seven American League pennants and their first four World Series championships. Meanwhile, the Red Sox have had four American League pennants but no World Series titles since dealing the "Sultan of

Swat." (Frazee sold the team to Bob Quinn in 1923, but Red Sox fans still blame Frazee and the "Curse of the Bambino" for the team's post-Ruth failures.)

Only team owned by successive pizza tycoons

Detroit Tigers

The Detroit Tigers changed hands October 10, 1992, but the source of the owner's wealth didn't when Little Caesars pizza baron Mike Ilitch paid $85 million to buy the Tigers from Domino's Pizza co-founder and owner Tom Monaghan. Monaghan had bought the Tigers in 1983, a year before they won their fourth World Series.

Value of biggest major league ownership deal

$978 million

Players get traded, but how about franchises? Well, before the 2002 season, there was a three-way deal involving majority ownership of two National League teams and an American League team. Montreal Expos owner Jeffrey Loria, who paid $75 million for it in 1999, sold the team for $120 million to Major League Baseball's 29 other owners after the Expos drew a league-worst 619,451 in 2001. Loria then turned around and bought the Florida Marlins for $158 million from John Henry. Henry then sold his 1 per cent interest in the New York Yankees to buy another American League legend, the Boston Red Sox, for $700 million. The trio of deals totaled $978 million.

CHAPTER 15

We Are Family

FAMILY TIES

"We Are Family" isn't just the name of the Pointer Sisters song adopted as the 1979 World Series champion Pittsburgh Pirates' theme. "We Are Family" is also a slogan that applies to baseball as a whole, because it's a game that unites fathers, sons, brothers, daughters, wives and mothers. And it's a game that reaffirms or reinvents relationships—sometimes in peculiar ways.

Most generations of a family to play Major League Baseball

3: Boone, Bell and Hairston clans

When Bret Boone debuted on August 19, 1992, 1-for-4 with an RBI in the Seattle Mariners' 10–8 win, the Boone clan became the first three-generation family to play in Major League Baseball. Bret's grandfather, Ray Boone, played for the Cleveland Indians from 1948 to 1960; his father, Bob, played from 1972 to 1990, and his brother, Aaron, debuted in 1997. Coincidentally, one of Bret's Seattle teammates in 2001 was David Bell, whose father, Buddy, and grandfather, Gus, were also major leaguers. The Hairstons are the only other baseball family in history to send three generations to the majors. Sam, Jerry Sr. and Jerry Jr. also have the distinction of being the first three-generation African-American family to play big league baseball.

First brothers to bat in order

Felipe, Matty and Jesus Alou, San Francisco, September 10, 1963

The Alou brothers—Jesus, Matty and Felipe—batted in order of ascending age for the San Francisco Giants in the eighth inning of a game in New York on September 10, 1963, though they were all unable to get the ball out of the infield. The brothers trio was also the first to play together in the outfield, in a game on September 22 that same year at Candlestick Park against the Mets. The Dominican Republic natives were also the first brothers with more than 1,000 career hits (Felipe had 2,101; Matty, 1,777, and Jesus, 1,216).

Only pitcher to allow home runs to all three Alou brothers

Ferguson Jenkins

Ferguson Jenkins is Canada's only Hall of Famer and the Alou brothers' favorite pitcher. He gave up home runs to all three of them. Jesus was first and last, homering for the San Francisco Giants on July 23, 1967, and for the Houston Astros on May 31, 1973; Felipe hit a four-bagger April 25, 1968, for the Braves; while Matty got his homer on September 5, 1971, for the St. Louis Cardinals.

First brothers to homer in the same National League game for opponents
Tony and Al Cuccinello, July 31, 1935
Joy ruled Long Island's Cuccinello clan on July 3, 1935. That's when Tony hit a homer for the Brooklyn Dodgers, who beat brother Al (also a home-run hitter) and the New York Giants 14–4.

Most prolific home-run-hitting brothers
Hank and Tommie Aaron
Although Tommie Aaron recorded only 13 career home runs, he and his brother, Hank Aaron, are baseball's most prolific slugging duo thanks to Hank's major league career record 755 homers. The Mobile, Alabama-born brothers played together from 1962 to 1971, including a game for the Milwaukee Braves on June 12, 1962, when they both homered against the Los Angeles Dodgers.

Most brothers to hit a major league home run
4: Ed, Jim, Frank and Joe Delahanty
The Delahanty family sent four Cleveland-born brothers to the big leagues—and they all hit home runs. Ed, Jim, Frank and Joe had a combined home-run total of 129. Hall of Famer Ed led with 101, Jim had 19 and Frank edged Joe five to four.

First African-American brothers in the major leagues

Moses Fleetwood Walker and Welday Walker

Jackie Robinson didn't break the color barrier, the Walker brothers did. In fact, Moses Fleetwood Walker was the first African-American player in the American Association when he caught for the Toledo Blue Stockings against the Louisville Eclipse on May 1, 1884. Moses had 40 hits and 23 runs in 42 games for a .263 average during his only season in a major league. His brother, Welday Walker, who joined him on the Blue Stockings on May 8 for a single game, had four hits and a run.

First brothers to play against each other in an All-Star game

Carlos and Lee May, July 23, 1969

May day came in July in 1969, when it was more than just an All-Star game between the American and National Leagues at Washington's R.F.K. Memorial Stadium. It was May versus May: Carlos for the National League and Lee for the American League. The brothers were also opponents in the 1971 All-Star game in Detroit.

Shortest career of a Hall of Famer's brother

0 pitches: Larry Yount, Houston, September 15, 1971

Evidently, the big leagues weren't big enough for two Younts. The baseball gods intervened just before Larry Yount was to debut on the mound for the Houston Astros in the ninth inning of a 4–2 loss to the Atlanta Braves. Yount was announced as the new pitcher, but injured his arm during warm-up. He was replaced, and never dealt a single major league pitch. His brother Robin debuted three years later with the Milwaukee Brewers and was inducted into the Hall of Fame in 1999.

Longest-running brother combination

14 years: Paul and Lloyd Waner, Pittsburgh

Hall of Fame brothers Paul and Lloyd Waner were inseparable
as well as teammates for 14 years on the Pittsburgh Pirates. Paul,
known as "Big Poison," was inducted in 1952. Lloyd, who was three
years younger, was known as "Little Poison"; he was enshrined in
1967. (The moniker "Poison" is "Brooklynese" for person.)

Most baseball-playing brothers on different teams, in different leagues, operated on in the same hospital—on the same day

2: Eric and Dale Soderholm, September 8, 1975

St. Mary's Hospital in Minneapolis cared for two baseball-playing
Soderholms on September 8, 1975. Eric, the Minnesota Twins'
third baseman, underwent surgery to remove cartilage from an
injured left knee and missed the entire 1976 season. His brother,
Dale, a third baseman with the Atlanta Braves International
League farm team in Richmond, Virginia, went under the knife
for foot surgery on the same day.

First baseball-playing twins convicted of battery

Jose and Ozzie Canseco

Jose and Ozzie Canseco, born July 2, 1964, in Havana, Cuba,
were briefly teammates with the 1990 Oakland Athletics. They
also teamed up after retirement in a Miami nightclub brawl on
October 31, 2001, and were convicted of battery in 2002. Both
twins spent time in jail in 2003—in separate cells, of course.

First brothers to pitch no-hitters

Bob and Ken Forsch

Bob Forsch upstaged his older brother, Ken, by being the first of
the pitching siblings to register a no-hitter. Bob, playing with the

Philadelphia Phillies, blanked the St. Louis Cardinals 5–0 on April 16, 1978. It would take Ken almost another year to get his no-hitter: a 6–0 Houston Astros win over the Atlanta Braves on April 7, 1979. Bob ended the tie with a second no-hitter on September 26, 1983, when he blanked the Montreal Expos 3–0. The brothers were both born in Sacramento, California.

First brothers to share a shutout

Rick and Paul Reuschel, Chicago (NL), August 21, 1975
Their mother always told Rick and Paul Reuschel to share, and they did their mother proud in 1975 when the Chicago Cubs pitching brothers from Quincy, Illinois, kept the Los Angeles Dodgers off the scoreboard in a 7–0 win at Wrigley Field. Rick was on his way to winning his 10th game of the season, but left after 6⅓ innings due to a blistered right hand. Paul came in to relieve him, and completed the shutout for his third win.

Only brothers to win two games each in the same World Series

Dizzy and Daffy Dean, St. Louis (NL), 1934
The 1934 World Series was the Dizzy and Daffy Show. Dizzy and Daffy Dean, that is—the St. Louis Cardinals who beat the Detroit Tigers in seven games with two wins each. Dizzy won Games 1 and 7. Daffy (known to his parents as Paul) won Games 3 and 6. The Deans were born in Lucas, Arkansas.

First brothers to pitch against each other

Jesse Barnes vs. Virgil Barnes, May 3, 1927
On May 3, 1927, a Barnes was bound to win, with Jesse Barnes of the Brooklyn Robins beating brother Virgil of the New York

Giants 7–6. The right-handed pitchers were teammates on the Giants from 1919 to 1923.

First pitcher to hit his only home run against his pitching brother
Joe Niekro, Houston, May 29, 1976

In 1976, Joe Niekro finally got revenge against his older brother, Phil, with a game-tying, seventh-inning homer for the Houston Astros. Joe also pitched eight innings for the 4–3 win over Phil's Atlanta Braves.

Most fathers and sons struck out by the same pitcher
15: Nolan Ryan

Nolan Ryan was a multi-generational strikeout artist. During his career, he struck out Sandy Alomar Sr. and his sons, Sandy Jr. and Roberto; Bobby Bonds and son, Barry; Tito Francona and son, Terry; Ken Griffey Sr. and Jr.; Hal McRae and son, Brian; Dick Schofield Sr. and Jr., and Maury Wills and son, Bump.

First catcher to use Scrabble to name his daughter
Bob Kearney, Seattle

Seattle Mariners catcher Bob Kearney wasn't looking for a double-word score on February 28, 1985, just a name for his newborn daughter. Kearney and his wife used a Scrabble crossword game to come up with the letters D-A-N-A, then took another vowel, the letter I. However, instead of calling the baby born February 28, 1985, Diana, they settled on Danai.

First woman drafted by a major league team
Karey Scheuler, Chicago White Sox

A father's love for his daughter is a special thing, particularly if the father is a major league general manager and the daughter plays hardball. Karey Scheuler was chosen in the 43rd round of 1993's draft by the Chicago White Sox. Scheuler's father was White Sox general manager Ron Scheuler. Karey never played a game "in the show," however.

First father and son to hit back-to-back home runs

Ken Griffey Sr. and Jr., Seattle, September 14, 1990
The two Ken Griffeys, who were both born in Donora, Pennsylvania, had back-to-back homers for the Seattle Mariners against the California Angels and pitcher Kirk McCaskill in 1990. Despite the father-and-son blasts, however, the Angels were 7–5 winners.

Most sons managed simultaneously by their father

2: Cal Ripken Jr. and Billy Ripken, Baltimore
The Baltimore Orioles had two Cal Ripkens in 1985: one in the dugout and one at shortstop, with Cal Ripken Sr. managing the O's to one victory in his only game at the helm. Two years later, there were three Ripkens: the two Cals and rookie second baseman Billy, though Ripken power didn't translate into wins. The team went 67–95, and Cal Sr.'s days with Baltimore were over the next season when he was fired after a dismal 0–8 start.

Only three-generation major league groundskeeping family

Bossard
Three generations of Bossards kept the diamonds gleaming at Chicago's Comiskey Park and Cleveland Municipal Stadium. And although their tactics were never questioned by the home team, visitors often complained. When Emil Bossard worked for the Indians in the 1920s and 1930s, for example, team owner Bill Veeck once asked him to move the outfield fences back 15 feet for

when the Yankees came to town—a move later ruled illegal by
the American League. His son, Gene Bossard, who worked at
Comiskey from 1940 to 1983, also altered the field to the White
Sox's advantage and stored balls in a room with a humidifier
to add up to one ounce to their weight. Roger was the third
generation of ballpark Bossards. His trick was ensuring that
the infield and bases were well watered to slow ground balls
and basestealers.

Age of youngest person to sing "Take Me Out to the Ball Game" at Wrigley Field
4: Darren Baker
The youngest son of Chicago Cubs manager Dusty Baker took the
microphone and led fans at Wrigley Field in "Take Me Out to the
Ball Game" on May 4, 2003. The tot's mother, Melissa, held him
on a countertop in the Cubs' press box so fans could see him sing
during the seventh-inning stretch. The 5–4 win over the Colorado
Rockies took place on "Dusty the Bear" Beanie Baby Day. The
first 10,000 fans received the doll, which resembled Darren's
famous father.

Longest probation for attacking a coach
5 years: the 15-year-old son of William Ligue Jr.
Like father, like son? Not quite. William Ligue Jr.'s 15-year-old
son, who can't be identified outside court, received five years' probation for joining his father in attacking Kansas City Royals first-
base coach Tom Gamboa on-field in the ninth inning of a White
Sox game in Chicago, September 19, 2002. The teenager was
banned from Comiskey Park, sent to mandatory counseling and
ordered to serve 30 hours of community service. Ligue, who
changed his plea to guilty on two counts of aggravated battery,
was given only 30 months probation.

Earliest ballplayer wedding

5 AM: Babe Ruth and Claire Hodgson, New York, April 17, 1929

Babe Ruth began his second marriage at the odd hour of 5 AM, when he wed actress Claire Hodgson at St. Gregory the Great Roman Catholic Church in New York. Why so early? The Yankees were scheduled to play that day, and the newlyweds wanted to avoid attention. But after two rainouts, the Yankees played their home opener the next day, with Ruth smacking a home run in honor of his new wife in the 7–3 win over the Boston Red Sox. Babe's estranged first wife, Helen, died in a fire on January 11, 1929.

Baseball's first husband-and-wife teammates

Jake and Kendall Burnham, San Angelo, Texas, May 14, 2003

Jake and Kendall Burnham were a team both on and off the diamond. On May 14, 2003, the husband and wife played together for the San Angelo Colts of the independent Central Baseball League in Texas, where Kendall struck out in her first at-bat on three straight pitches as a pinch-hitter to end an 8–1 loss to the Amarillo Colts. Her newlywed husband, Jake, was the third baseman. The former Kendall Richards was a star softball player in college and played pro fast pitch in 1999 and 2000.

Only trade of wives in major league history

Marilyn Peterson for Susan Kekich, March 5, 1973

Fritz Peterson and Mike Kekich were teammates with the New York Yankees, but they weren't happy with their "home teams." So the two couples literally traded families—including their dogs. (Susan did keep her daughters Kristen and Regan; Marilyn kept her sons Gregg and Eric.) On June 12, Kekich was traded to the Indians for Lowell Palmer. Peterson met Marilyn Monks at Northern Illinois University, and the couple married in December 1964; the Kekiches were high-school sweethearts.

Most famous baseball marriage
Joe DiMaggio and Marilyn Monroe, January 14, 1954
Joe DiMaggio was in his third year of retirement, but he didn't stay out of the public eye for long. He tied the knot with blonde bombshell Marilyn Monroe in San Francisco on January 14, 1954, a year before his election to baseball's Hall of Fame.

Most famous ballplayer divorce
Joe DiMaggio and Marilyn Monroe, October 27, 1954
Their divorce received as much press as their marriage, but the breakup was more public than the courtship. In Santa Monica Superior Court, Monroe said she hoped to gain love, warmth, affection and understanding from her marriage with DiMaggio. "But the relationship turned out to be one of coldness and indifference," she said. Although DiMaggio and Monroe's partnership lasted only nine months, his love for her lasted until the end of his life. When Monroe died in 1962 and was buried in Los Angeles, DiMaggio arranged to have a bouquet of roses delivered to her crypt every week until he died in 1999.

Most known relationships with heiresses and showbiz women during pitching career
10: Bo Belinsky
Pitcher Bo Belinsky had an unremarkable 28–51 record in eight major league seasons with five teams. But his exploits with the ladies were legendary. He had both long and short relationships with many equally famous women at the dawn of the 1960s sexual

revolution, including a marriage to *Playboy*'s 1965 Playmate of the Year, Jo Collins, and heiress Jane Weyerhaeuser. Belinsky also dated actresses Ann-Margret, Paulette Goddard, Tina Louise, Juliet Prowse and Mamie Van Doren; singer Connie Stevens; ex-Iranian Queen Sorraya, and heiress Doris Duke.

Most unrelated Hermans in one game

2: *Billy and Babe Herman, Chicago (NL), August 19, 1933*
Billy Herman of Albany, Indiana, was the second baseman and Floyd Caves "Babe" Herman, from Buffalo, New York, was the rightfielder when the Chicago Cubs visited the New York Giants in 1933. There were only three Hermans in baseball history and two were teammates (Pitcher Art Herman of Louisville was the third). But what made the game even more significant was the appearance of relief pitcher Leroy Herrmann, whose name sounded the same but included two extra consonants. The Giants were 8–4 winners.

Most children of a pitcher with first names beginning with the letter K

4: *Koby, Kory, Kacy and Kody Clemens*
Pitching great Roger Clemens liked issuing strikeouts to batters he faced. Twice in his career he mowed down 20 in a game. So it's no surprise that he chose to give each of his four sons a name beginning with the letter "K" — scorekeeper shorthand for a strikeout.

Most children born on the same day to a major leaguer via in-vitro fertilization

3: *Dave Righetti, July 19, 1991*
Pitcher Dave Righetti and his wife, Kandice, scored a rare triple play in 1991, when Kandice's sister acted as surrogate mother and

gave birth to the couple's triplets: girls Nicolette and Natalee, and son, Wesley.

First relative of Elvis Presley signed by a major league club

Kirk Presley, New York (NL), August 28, 1993
The New York Mets know what it's like in heartbreak hotel. Their top draft pick in 1993 was Elvis Presley's cousin, Kirk, signed on August 28 and given a $960,000 bonus. But this Presley never became a King on the diamond. In fact, he didn't get beyond class A in the minors.

Most home runs by a son against a team managed by his father

6: Moises Alou
Parental pride has its limits when the opposing team's slugger is your own son. Felipe Alou has watched his leftfielder son, Moises, homer six times against his teams. It happened against manager Felipe's Montreal Expos twice in 1998, and once in 2000 and again in 2001 when Moises was with the Houston Astros. Moises hit another two in 2003 as a Chicago Cub when his dad was the skipper of the San Francisco Giants.

Only major leaguer to miss a game to watch his fiancé play in soccer's World Cup

Nomar Garciaparra, Boston
His Boston Red Sox were the American League's playoff-bound wildcard team before they played the Tampa Bay Devil Rays on closing day of the 2003 regular season. Still, star shortstop Nomar Garciaparra received permission to leave the team for a day to

watch his fiancé, Mia Hamm, play for the United States against North Korea in the FIFA Women's World Cup in Columbus, Ohio. The defending champion Americans had already advanced to the quarterfinal, so superstar Hamm was benched to avoid injury, then led her team to third place in the tournament. Garciaparra, who missed his team's 3–1 loss to the Devil Rays in Tampa Bay, broke out of a slump in the American League championship but failed to lift the Red Sox beyond the New York Yankees and into the 2003 World Series.

Longest hunger strike in support of a slumping brother
17 days: Frank Slaton
Jim Slaton's third season with the California Angels was anything but a charm, so Slaton's brother, Frank, tried to help the right-handed pitcher snap his slump by going on a hunger strike. The Slaton sibling swore off solid food on June 13, 1986, and said he wouldn't munch another morsel until his brother won or saved a game. The hunger strike eventually did end, but not because of its success. The Angels had released Jim, who still hadn't managed a win or save; picked up by the Detroit Tigers, he finished his career with two saves. As for Frank, he did win something at the losing game. The hunger strike made him 16 pounds lighter.

CHAPTER 16

A Game for the Ages

SPANNING THE GENERATIONS

Baseball is a game for the ages: for the young and for the old. It bridges the generations, from the wins and losses of yesteryear to our hopes and dreams for the future. And it gives us a chance to be young again. The human race may never invent a time machine, but the next best thing is baseball.

Age of youngest major leaguer

15: Joe Nuxhall, Cincinnati

Joe Nuxhall wasn't old enough to drive a car, but the southpaw was good enough to wear a Cincinnati Reds uniform on June 10, 1944. Nuxhall, born July 30, 1928, pitched two-thirds of an inning in the 18–0 loss to the St. Louis Cardinals. He had signed a major league contract while still in high school, but didn't become a regular until 1952, at the ripe old age of 23.

Age of oldest player to get a hit

53: Minnie Minoso, Chicago (AL)

Talk about a generation gap. California Angels pitcher Sid Monge was just eight days shy of his second birthday when Cuba-born Minnie Minoso debuted with the Cleveland Indians in 1949. But when Minoso was 53 and a designated hitter with the Chicago White Sox, he hit Monge's first pitch on September 12, 1976. Minoso didn't see action again until 1980, when he went 0–for–2 in two games for the White Sox. The 58-year-old and Nick Altrock are the only five-decade major leaguers.

Age of youngest home run hitter

17: Tommy Brown, Brooklyn

Tommy Brown was still a hometown boy when he hit his first home run for the Brooklyn Dodgers on August 20, 1945. The Brooklyn native, born December 6, 1927, blasted a pitch from Pittsburgh Pirate Preacher Roe over the wall in the 11–1 Dodgers win.

Only players to hit major league home runs before age 20 and after age 40

Ty Cobb and Rusty Staub

Not only did their last names rhyme, but they also stood the test of time. Ty Cobb—born December 18, 1886—hit his first home run in 1905 and his last in 1928. Rusty Staub, who was born April 1, 1944, and had six home runs in his 1963 rookie campaign, ended his career with one for the Mets in 1985.

Age of oldest rookie

42: Satchel Paige, Cleveland

Satchel Paige had already had a full career in the Negro Leagues when Cleveland Indians owner Bill Veeck discovered him. Paige, who signed with the Indians in 1948, debuted in a 5–3 loss on July 9 to the St. Louis Browns just two days after his 42nd birthday. Paige retired after the 1953 season with the Browns, but came out of retirement on September 25, 1965, to pitch three innings for the Kansas City Athletics. He was 59. Paige gave up only a double to Boston Red Sox Carl Yastrzemski in the 5–2 A's loss.

Age of youngest perfect-game pitcher

22: Jim "Catfish" Hunter, Oakland, May 8, 1968

"Catfish" Hunter was exactly a month into his 23rd year when he pitched a perfect game for the Oakland Athletics against the Minnesota Twins. The A's 4–0 win was the ninth perfect game in baseball history.

Age of youngest manager

23: Roger Peckinpaugh, New York (AL)

Roger Peckinpaugh's managerial debut was a baptism by fire, when he succeeded Frank Chance in the New York Yankees dugout on September 16, 1914, and ended the season 10–10. Peckinpaugh, born February 5, 1891, didn't get another managing gig until the Cleveland Indians hired him 14 years later. When he retired in 1941, his successor was 24-year-old Lou Boudreau. The Tribe won the 1948 World Series when Boudreau was just 31.

Age of oldest manager

88: Connie Mack, Philadelphia (AL)

Connie Mack was still managing the Philadelphia Athletics when most people his age were enjoying retirement and the company of their grandchildren. In fact, Mack's players were young enough to be his grandchildren when the 88-year-old managed the Athletics to a 52–102 record in 1950, his final season before retirement.

Age of youngest general manager

28: Theo Epstein, Boston

Boston Red Sox pitcher John Burkett felt much older than his 38 years in 2003. His boss, general manager Theo Epstein, was 10 years his junior. Epstein, who became general manager in 2002 and saw the Red Sox come within five outs of winning 2003's American League pennant, got his start as an intern with the Baltimore Orioles' media relations office in 1992. When the Red Sox offered him a job as assistant general manager, he was director of baseball operations for the San Diego Padres.

Most trades after age 40

4: Jesse Orosco

It was about time for Jesse Orosco's arrival in Minneapolis-St. Paul, Minnesota. The 46-year-old was drafted by the Twins in 1978, but didn't show up until 2003 after a trade from the New York Yankees for pitcher Juan Padilla. By then, Orosco was no rookie. The Santa Barbara, California-native was a seasoned veteran relief pitcher who pitched the final out of the 1986 World Series for the New York Mets. It was Orosco's fourth trade since 1999, when the Baltimore Orioles returned him to the Mets for

Chuck McElroy. The Mets then sent him to St. Louis for Cardinal Joe McEwing during spring training in 2000. The Yankees picked him up on July 22, 2003, from the San Diego Padres, hoping to shore up their bullpen for a playoff run.

Age of oldest player to be traded

48: Phil Niekro

Phil Niekro was no spring chicken when he became a Toronto Blue Jay in the summer of 1987. The Cleveland Indians dealt him to Toronto on August 9 for Darryl Landrum and Don Gordon. Niekro, a native of Blaine, Ohio, retired after his 24th big league season.

Most no-hitters after turning 40

2: Nolan Ryan

Lordy, Lordy, look what Nolan did after he turned 40. Baseball's greatest fastballer just seemed to improve with age, throwing no-hitter number six at age 43 for the Texas Rangers in a 5–0 win over the Oakland Athletics on June 11, 1990. Not even a year later, on May 1, 1991, he did it again, breaking his own record for oldest no-hit pitcher by blanking the Toronto Blue Jays 3–0. (By comparison, Cy Young's last no-hitter came at age 41.) Ryan would pitch a record 27 years in the majors with the New York Mets, California Angels, Houston Astros and Rangers. And although he never won the Cy Young Award, he did hurl in eight All-Star games.

CHAPTER 17

Team Works, Perks and Jerks

ALL FOR ONE

There's no "I" in team—unless, of course, your team is the Indians. But seriously, a team is a special unit where the whole is greater than the sum of its parts. That is, until the team comes apart, because a team united can become a team untied. All it takes is a few loose parts.

First game played by a professional baseball team

Cincinnati vs. Mansfield: June 1, 1869

The Mansfield Independents should have been called the Amateurs the day they went up against the Cincinnati Red Stockings. By the time the game was over, baseball's first professional nine from Cincinnati had more than earned their wages with their 48–14 win. Of course, manager Harry Wright, who doubled as centerfielder and relief pitcher, only earned $1,200 in 1869; his 22-year-old brother, shortstop George Wright, had the biggest paycheck, $1,400—but the Red Stockings' entire payroll was only $9,400. These days, most major leaguers earn that much per game.

Oldest professional sports league in North America

National League

They don't call it the "senior circuit" for nothing. The National League began play on April 22, 1876, when the Boston Red Stockings beat the host Philadelphia Athletics 6–5. "Orator" Jim O'Rourke was the first safe hitter, while Joseph Borden got the win on the mound. The National League was the successor of the National Association, which folded in 1875 after its fifth season.

Most consecutive wins

26: New York (NL), 1916

September 1916 was a glorious month for the New York Giants. Too bad there was no October at the Polo Grounds, because the Giants finished fourth in the National League. The streak began September 7 with a 4–1 win over the Brooklyn Robins. But all the fun ended September 30 when the Boston Braves were 8–3 winners in the second game of a doubleheader.

Most consecutive losses

24: Cleveland (NL), 1899

The Cleveland Spiders spun a web of defeat when they lost two-dozen games in a row from August 26 to September 18, 1899.

Worst winning percentage

.130: Cleveland (NL), 1899

The Cleveland Spiders are baseball legends for all the wrong reasons: they finished 1899 with a record 134 losses—including the final two-game series against their Ohio rivals, the Cincinnati Reds—and, during their last 41 games, the Spiders could only muster one victory for a total of 20 wins. The Spiders were also outscored 1,242 to 529, and their pitching ace (if you could call him that), Jim Huey, fashioned a record of four wins and 30 losses. All in all, the Spiders compiled the all-time worst winning percentage of .130. Conversely, their losing percentage was .870.

First cigar-smoking protest on closing day

Cincinnati, October 4, 1902

The Cincinnati Reds were 33½ games behind the first-place Pittsburgh Pirates and desperately wanted to the end their disastrous 1902 season early. More specifically, they wanted to forfeit their last game against the Pirates. Reds owner Barney Dreyfuss overruled the players, who resorted to smoking cigars on the field, but regretted the decision when the Pirates were 11–2 winners. Dreyfuss was so embarassed he offered refunds to ticket holders.

Most runs before the first out

10: Boston, June 27, 2003

The Florida Marlins were wondering when the punishment would ever end when they met the Boston Red Sox at Fenway Park for an interleague game on June 27, 2003. The Red Sox had an American League record 14-run first inning—10 of them registered before the game's first out. Marlins Carl Pavano, Michael Tejera and Allen Levrault combined for 91 pitches in the 50-minute first inning. The Red Sox coasted to a 25–8 win.

Most shutouts suffered in a week

4: Chicago (NL), 1968

The Chicago Cubs should have gone into hibernation during the last week of spring 1968. Between June 15 and 21, they were shut out four times: once by the Atlanta Braves and three times by the St. Louis Cardinals. Billy Williams broke the streak by driving in the winning run with a sacrifice fly in the third inning of a 3–2 road victory over the Cincinnati Reds.

Most consecutive days rained out

10: Philadelphia (NL), 1909

The 1909 Philadelphia Phillies got used to carrying umbrellas when Mother Nature wreaked havoc with their schedule. For 10 consecutive days, the Phillies were kept off the field by rain.

Most players used in a regular-season game

54: Seattle vs. Texas, September 25, 1992

Why not let everyone play? That's what the Seattle Mariners and Texas Rangers virtually did in a 1992 game, when the Mariners won the 16-inning game 4–3 on the strength of 29 players, including 11 pitchers. The Rangers used 25.

Most runs in a major league game

49: Chicago vs. Philadelphia, August 25, 1922

The Chicago Cubs took advantage of 14 runs in the fourth inning to beat the Philadelphia Phillies 26–23—the highest-scoring game in major league history.

Most innings in a scoreless American League game

18: Detroit vs. Washington, July 16, 1909

When the Detroit Tigers and Washington Senators battled 18 innings on July 16, 1909, not only did they fail to settle a winner, neither team scored a run. It was such a weird game that Ty Cobb—baseball's all-time hit king until Pete Rose—went hitless in seven at-bats. The game was eventually suspended due to darkness.

Most players involved in a single trade

19: New York (AL) and Baltimore, November 18, 1954

The New York Yankees and Baltimore Orioles were never the same after the 1954 season. For on November 18 they began a mammoth trade involving 17 players, plus two to be named at a later date. Pitcher Mike Blyzka, outfielder Jim Fridley, shortstop Billy Hunter, first baseman Dick Kryhoski, pitcher Don Larsen, catcher Darrell Johnson and pitcher Bob Turley left the O's for the Big Apple. Going the other way were pitcher Harry Byrd, outfielder Ted Del Guercio, second baseman Don Leppert, pitcher Jim McDonald, outfielder Bill Miller, shortstop Willie Miranda, infielder Kal Segrist, catchers Hal Smith and Gus Triandos and outfielder Gene Woodling.

Most convincing April Fool's Day trade prankster

Kurt Bevacqua, San Diego, April 1, 1985

Infielder Kurt Bevacqua cooked up a blockbuster prank to play on his San Diego KBZT listeners during his spring training reports on April 1, 1985. The Padre reported that first baseman Jim Flannery had been sent to the Milwaukee Brewers for Rollie Fingers—flipped for first baseman Steve Garvey and rookie outfielder Jerry Davis to the New York Yankees—in return for Don Mattingly, Willie Randolph and a minor league pitcher. Bevacqua gave no hint that he was fooling, and outraged fans deluged the radio station's phone lines to offer their opinions on the deal.

Biggest payroll for a major league team

$180.3 million: New York (AL), 2003

The New York Yankees paid players a record $180.3 million in 2003 according to figures submitted to the commissioner's office. On the other end of the scale, the Tampa Bay Devil Rays had a modest $31.6-million payroll.

Biggest contract

$252 million: Alex Rodriguez, Texas

The Texas Rangers made Alex Rodriguez baseball's first quarter-billion-dollar man when A-Rod went shopping for the best deal after his contract with the Seattle Mariners expired in 2000. The Rangers offered Rodriguez $252 million over 10 years and signed the New York-born shortstop on December 11.

Most times a city got a new team during spring training

2: Milwaukee

The Boston Braves decided to play the 1953 National League season in Milwaukee—a move they announced on March 18, 1953. Meanwhile, the Braves ended up in Atlanta in 1966. Milwaukee then went without a team until 1970's spring training, when the American League's year-old Seattle Pilots moved to Milwaukee and became the Brewers—less than a week before Opening Day.

Last team to break the color barrier

Boston Red Sox

When Elijah "Pumpsie" Green was recalled from Minneapolis by the Boston Red Sox on July 21, 1959, the Red Sox completed what the Brooklyn Dodgers had begun 12 years earlier: 20th-century racial integration in the majors. The infielder from Oakland, California, played four years for the Red Sox before ending his career with the New York Mets in 1963.

Most years of spring training on an island

30: *Chicago* (NL)
The Chicago Cubs called the "Isle with a Smile" their spring training home for 30 years, beginning in 1921. Chewing gum tycoon William Wrigley Jr., who bought the Cubs in 1916, paid $3 million for property on Catalina Island, just off Los Angeles, where he built a diamond and practice field near his country club at Avalon. The team returned to the mainland when a freak snowfall marred spring training in 1951. The Cubs now train in Mesa, Arizona.

Most players suspended

16: *Chicago* (AL) *vs. Detroit, April 27, 2000*
Major League Baseball was anything but sweet when it disciplined 16 White Sox and Tigers in April 2000. The combined 82 games of suspensions were levied after the Chicago White Sox and Detroit Tigers brawled twice in an April 22, 2000, game, with seven batters hit during the 14–6 White Sox win. Detroit manager Phil Garner and Chicago manager Jerry Manuel were suspended eight games each, and Tigers coach Juan Samuel received 15 games for his role in the mêlée.

Most players lost after a team bus stall

2: *Gene Conley and Elijah "Pumpsie" Green, Boston, July 26, 1962*
The Boston Red Sox were happy to escape from New York after losing 13–3 to the Yankees in July 1962, but two players in particular were eager to depart the Big Apple. When the team bus stalled for 15 minutes near the George Washington Bridge, Gene Conley and Elijah "Pumpsie" Green disappeared. Conley hailed a cab to

Idlewild Airport, where he was refused entry to an El Al flight to Israel, and turned up 68 hours later near Boston, where he lived. Green was gone for just over a day.

Most players found playing table tennis by a private detective

2: Tony Kubek and Bobby Richardson, New York (AL), September 15, 1958

New York Yankees general manager George Weiss always wondered what his players did after they skedaddled from Yankee Stadium. So he hired a detective, who discovered that two of them just played with paddles. The private detective Weiss hired to follow Tony Kubek and Bobby Richardson reported finding them playing table tennis at a YMCA.

Most major leaguers found dead in Canada

2: Ed Delahanty, 1903, and Len Koenecke, 1935

Two drunk and distraught major leaguers met their demise on trains and planes in Canada. On July 2, 1903, Ed Delahanty deserted his Washington Senators teammates, and a train conductor ejected the drunk and disorderly player near Niagara Falls, Ontario, instead of calling police. Delahanty walked along the railway tracks, but fell off a bridge and drowned going over Niagara Falls. The 35-year-old's body was found a week later. Len Koenecke, who was released by the Brooklyn Dodgers on September 15, 1935, was subsequently kicked off an American Airlines flight in Detroit for drunkenness. But he chartered a plane for Buffalo, continued to be unruly and threatened to grab the aircraft's controls. The pilots subdued him with a fire extinguisher— causing a fatal blow to the head, then landed in Toronto.

Worst case of mistaken identity by a baseball card manufacturer

Confusing Ken Hubbs with Dick Ellsworth, 1966

Ken Hubbs played only three years as a second baseman for the Chicago Cubs, yet after he died in a 1964 plane crash near Provo, Utah, his image lived on. By mistake, Hubbs's photo was placed on Cubs teammate Dick Ellsworth's card in the Topps-manufactured 1966 set (number 447).

Most expansion-team ballplayers stuck in an elevator

16: New York (NL), April 10, 1962

The New York Mets had nowhere to go but down on the eve of their inaugural National League season, when 16 players were stuck in a malfunctioning elevator at the St. Louis Chase Hotel for 20 minutes, the night before they played the Cardinals.

Most disastrous community relations promotion

Strike Out Domestic Violence Night, Durham, North Carolina, May 22, 1995

Do as we say, not as we do. That was the underlying theme one night in 1995 at Durham Athletic Park, when the class A Durham Bulls sponsored Strike Out Domestic Violence Night. The event was marred by a half-hour brawl between the Bulls and the opposing Winston-Salem Warthogs after Bull Earl Nelson kicked Warthog Glenn Cullop in the groin and head, breaking his jaw. Nelson was suspended for six games.

Worst "minor" injury suffered in a clubhouse brawl

Sprained thumb ligament: Rich "Goose" Gossage, April 19, 1979

It sounds small, but the sprained left thumb ligament "Goose" Gossage suffered in 1979 caused a big problem for the New York Yankees relief pitcher. It kept him out of play for almost three months. Gossage suffered the injury during a fight with teammate Cliff Johnson after the Yankees lost 6–3 to the Baltimore Orioles. The Yankees had to wait for Gossage's digit to mend, but then gave the finger to Johnson on June 15, dealing him to the Cleveland Indians. Manager Billy Martin never forgave Johnson. He even paid rookie Bob Kammeyer $100 to hit the former Yankee with a pitch during the Yankees' 16–3 win over the Indians on September 18.

Only pro-earrings protest thwarted by a manager
Los Angeles, May 18, 1994
Cincinnati Reds owner Marge Schott was constantly creating controversy. She once told a newspaper reporter, for example, that "only fruits wear earrings." So on May 18, 1994, Los Angeles Dodgers pitcher Roger McDowell brought enough earrings to equip his team in the Riverfront Stadium clubhouse in Cincinnati. McDowell lobbied the players to wear them in a game, but manager Tommy Lasorda had the last word: "No."

Most controversial haircut
Rey Sanchez, New York (NL), May 6, 2003
Never has a haircut caused so much trouble for the New York Mets than the one Rey Sanchez got during an away game in 2003. The Mets even had a team meeting to ask Sanchez why he couldn't have waited until after the game. Sanchez, who got a trim from a clubhouse attendant during a loss to the St. Louis Cardinals, was already under fire for a slow start to the season after registering a lowly .141 average for April.

Earliest news conference to announce a retirement
5 AM: Tony Conigliaro, July 11, 1971
California Angel Tony Conigliaro wanted to get his career over with bright and early by calling a 5 AM news conference to announce his

retirement. He was only 26 when his failing eyesight made it impossible for him to continue playing the game he loved. A star at 19 with the Red Sox, Conigliaro's troubles began when he was hit by a pitch in 1967, causing loss of depth perception and a blind spot. But he did come back after one year out of the game, with 20 home runs in 1969 and 36 in 1970 before he was traded to California.

Most cities visited in fewest days

Five cities in five days: Chicago (NL), 1907

The Cubs were on the prowl in 1907, playing games in five cities over five days. But it wasn't a fruitful hunt in terms of victories — they had only two in the seven-game stretch. The Cubs' journey began on August 29, 1907, in Brooklyn, where they shut out their hosts 5–0. Next stop, Pittsburgh, for an August 30 doubleheader. The Cubs lost 2–1 but beat the Pirates 6–0 in the nightcap. They then closed out August with a 2–1 win over the Reds in Cincinnati and came home to open September with a 7–2 loss to the St. Louis Cardinals. The travel-weary Cubs followed the Cardinals to St. Louis on September 2, but lost 6–0 and 9–0 in a doubleheader.

Most pairs of underwear bought for a road trip

25: Orlando Cabrera, Montreal, 2003

Orlando Cabrera likes his fresh every day — and we're not talking Montreal's famous bagels. In 2003, the Montreal Expos shortstop bought 25 pairs of new underwear before his team departed for the longest-distance regular-season road trip in the game's history. The six-city, 25-day journey covered 11,310 miles and 22 games — in Miami, Philadelphia, Seattle, Oakland, Pittsburgh and San Juan, Puerto Rico, the Expos' second home in 2003. But it wasn't the Expos' longest absence from Olympic Stadium. In 1991, they played the final 26 games of the season on the road after a 55-ton concrete beam fell from the stadium roof.

Longest road trip

50 games: Cleveland Spiders, 1899

The Cleveland Spiders were so bad in 1899 — losing all but six games of a 50-game, 53-day road trip — that their fans didn't want to see them play at home. The Spiders came home for a week, but then returned to the road for more punishment. This time, they actually won once during the 36-game, 46-day misadventure.

Longest city-to-city walk by a baseball broadcaster

315 miles: Jim Rooker, Philadelphia to Pittsburgh, 1989

Play-by-play broadcaster Jim Rooker put his feet in his mouth on June 8, 1989, when the ex-Pittsburgh Pirates pitcher told listeners that he would walk home if the Bucs lost their 10–0 lead in Philadelphia. The Pirates scored just one more run, but the Phillies countered with 15. And when the season was over, Rooker stayed true to his word and walked 315 miles between the Pennsylvania cities in 12 days.

Most lopsided shutout

28-0: Providence vs. Philadelphia, August 21, 1883

Quakers are known for their generosity. And the same is true of the Philadelphia baseball team of the same name. The Providence Grays, managed by professional baseball pioneer Harry Wright, crushed the Philadelphia Quakers 28–0 in a 1883 National League matchup.

Longest shutout

24 innings: Houston vs. New York (NL), April 15, 1968

The Mets took a beating on April 15, 1968, when the team from Flushing Meadows, Queens, got flushed in a 1–0 loss to the Houston Astros. The Mets had two-dozen innings to score a run, but failed.

Longest game in baseball history

33 innings: Pawtucket vs. Rochester, April 18 to 19 and June 23, 1981

What a bargain! If you were among the last 20 fans at Pawtucket's McCoy Stadium on April 19, 1981, not only had you seen 32 innings of baseball but you got a 1981 season's pass for enduring the longest game in baseball history. The eight-hour, six-minute marathon between the Pawtucket Red Sox and Rochester Red Wings started with 1,740 fans at 8 PM on April 18. It was finally suspended at 4:07 AM with the score tied 2–2, April 19, after International League president Harold Cooper telephoned the umpires (who were shocked to learn that they should not have started any new innings after 12:50 AM). Pawtucket's Dave Koza broke the tie with a bases loaded single when the game resumed June 23 in the 33rd inning.

Most games between two teams in a season

26 games: New York and Boston, 2003

We've got to stop meeting like this! The New York Yankees and Boston Red Sox played a record 26 times in 2003, with New York winning the regular-season series 10–9 and the playoff matchup 4–3. But the last win was the most important: the Yankees beat Boston 6–5 in 11 innings on October 16 for the American League championship and a World Series berth.

Last three-team doubleheader

St. Louis, New York, Boston (NL): September 13, 1951

It was bonus baseball with bonus teams in St. Louis in 1951, when the Cardinals hosted a doubleheader with two different teams.

They beat the New York Giants 6–4 in an afternoon game to compensate for a rainout, then lost 2–0 to the Boston Braves in the regularly scheduled night game. That was the last time a team has ever played two different opponents on the same day.

Most players to take the wrong train with an opposing team

2: Ski Melillo and Eric McNair, Boston (AL), 1937

The Boston Red Sox were without infielders Ski "Spinach" Melillo and Eric McNair when their train to New York left Boston after a doubleheader sweep of the Philadelphia Athletics on July 4, 1937. It turned out Melillo and McNair were napping on a train carrying the Athletics to Washington, D.C. The pair didn't discover that they had boarded the wrong car until the next morning. The Red Sox were on track to play the Yankees, but the A's were heading to a series with the Senators.

Most players to avoid a team's maiden flight

2: Mark Koenig and Jim Bottomley, Cincinnati, 1934

The Cincinnati Reds became the first major league team to fly on a commercial airliner on June 7, 1934, after losing 2–1 to the Pittsburgh Pirates at home. But they had two aviophobes on the roster. Infielder Mark Koenig and first baseman Jim Bottomley were too scared to travel by air, so they took the train instead for the June 8 game against the Cubs in Chicago, which the Reds won 4–3.

CHAPTER 18

Midsummer Night's Dreaming

A GALAXY OF SHINING

ALL-STARS

For more than 70 years, baseball has paused, ever so conveniently, in the middle of the season and the middle of summer. During this lull in the regular season, competition is put aside for a day while the biggest talents in the game join forces for the ultimate exhibition contest: the All-Star game.

First "All-Star" game

Cleveland Naps vs. American League selects, July 24, 1911

It was a hastily organized affair, but ballplayers felt that they had to do something after the Naps' 31-year-old star pitcher, Adie Joss, died suddenly on April 14, leaving behind a wife and two children. On a day off, Joss's friends and foes alike gathered for the benefit ball game that, by default, was baseball's first Midsummer Classic. That initial game drew 15,000 people to Cleveland's League Park and featured nine future Hall of Famers: Ty Cobb, Tris Speaker, Frank "Home Run" Baker, Eddie Collins, Walter Johnson, Bobby Wallace and Sam Crawford on the AL team and Cleveland's Nap Lajoie and Cy Young. The visiting All-Stars were 5–3 winners. (Joss was enshrined in the Hall of Fame in 1978.)

First American League vs. National League All-Star game

Comiskey Park, Chicago, July 6, 1933

Just this once, *Chicago Tribune* sports editor Arch Ward got the story he wanted, while baseball fans got to see all of the game's best players on the same diamond. It was all Ward's idea: an exhibition game with the best players from each league at Comiskey Park—to coincide with the 1933 Chicago World's Fair. It was a remarkable game. New York Yankees pitcher Lefty Gomez had the first All-Star RBI—a second-inning single that scored Jimmie Dykes—and led the American League to a 4–2 win over the National League. The All-Star game became an annual, crowd-pleasing affair.

First indoor All-Star game

Astrodome, Houston, July 9, 1968

Houston's Astrodome is a grand building, but the first All-Star game held there was not a grand affair. In fact, all the scoring happened in the bottom of the first while Willie Mays made his way around the bases in almost every conceivable fashion. For starters, Mays got to first on a fielding error, then advanced to second on a wild pitch and third on a single—then scored after a double play. The National League delighted the crowd with a 1–0 win.

Longest All-Star game
15 innings: July 11, 1967
All-Star baseball is America's biggest annual summertime TV sports showcase, which means commercials—lots of commercials. The team managers substitute freely on the mound, at the plate and in the field, giving as many players as possible their chance to shine. But the teams took it to the limit in 1967, when Tony Perez broke a 1–1 tie with a solo home run in the top of the 15th inning for the National League. Tom Seaver pitched the final three outs of the three-hour, 41-minute marathon.

Fastest All-Star game
One hour, 53 minutes: July 9, 1940
The National League cooked up a winner in 1940, when it scored three runs in the first inning and allowed only three hits at Sportsman's Park in St. Louis. The senior circuit blanked the American League 4–0.

Largest All-Star game attendance
72,086: Cleveland, August 9, 1981
The 1981 Midsummer Classic was a classic, but, for the first time in its history, it wasn't held in midsummer. When the players association's strike ended, the season resumed at Cleveland's Municipal Stadium, where a record crowd watched Montreal Expo Gary Carter hit a pair of home runs in the National League's 5–4 win.

Most All-Star game appearances for one league

24: Stan Musial and Willie Mays
St. Louis Cardinal "Stan the Man" Musial and San Francisco Giant "Say Hey" Willie Mays played two-dozen times each for the National League. The National League won 17 times with Mays.

Most appearances on the losing All-Star team

15: Brooks Robinson
Third baseman Brooks Robinson spent his entire career with the Baltimore Orioles. It didn't matter a bit to Hall of Fame voters that he played on 15 losing teams with the American League All-Stars.

Most All-Star games managed

10: Casey Stengel
Nobody votes for the All-Star managers — it's up to their teams to get them the gig. And thanks to the New York Yankees' perennial World Series appearances, manager Casey Stengel found himself leading the American League All-Stars 10 times. Stengel's managerial record was 4–6.

Most All-Star wins managed

7: Walter Alston
Walter Alston struck out in his only major league at-bat on September 27, 1936, but he did enjoy a 23-year career managing the Dodgers in Brooklyn and Los Angeles. Alston, who picked up four World Series rings, managed the National League to seven All-Star victories.

First pitcher to win three All-Star games

Lefty Gomez: 1933, 1935 and 1937
His New York Yankees teammates thought he was an oddball. And Lefty Gomez certainly did have a goofy imagination. He thought

it was a good idea for goldfish to have revolving bowls so they could swim less, for example. However, Gomez was lucky enough to be on the inside looking out for the American League, and won three All-Star games (all in odd years). He won the inaugural Midsummer Classic in Chicago on July 6, 1933, repeated the feat two years later in Cleveland and completed the hat trick in Washington, D.C., in 1937.

Most consecutive strikeouts to start the All-Star game
4: Pedro Martinez, July 13, 1999
Having the home-field advantage meant everything to Boston Red Sox ace Pedro Martinez during the 1999 All-Star game at Boston's Fenway Park. The Red Sox pitcher fanned the National League's first four batters: Barry Larkin, Larry Walker, Sammy Sosa and Mark McGwire. Martinez would garner one more strikeout in the American League's 4–1 win.

First National League write-in candidate to start the All-Star game
Rico Carty, July 14, 1970
Outfielder Rico Carty was cursed. He came one point shy of being a career .300 hitter, and, in 1971, his underinsured Atlanta barbeque restaurant burned down. But Atlanta fans loved him. Carty was integral to the Braves' 1969 National League West division championship, and fans rewarded him by electing him as a write-in candidate to the All-Star game at Cincinnati's Riverfront Stadium. The NL won 5–4 in 12 innings.

Most players pulled from an All-Star game starting lineup
2: George Crowe and Wally Post, Cincinnati, June 28, 1957
George Crowe and Wally Post were falling stars in the summer of 1957, when Cincinnati fans were stuffing ballot boxes, hoping to

paint the National League All-Stars "Red." But the campaign was thwarted. Commissioner Ford Frick replaced Crowe and Post with Willie Mays and Hank Aaron in the starting lineup at Sportsman's Park, St. Louis. Cardinal Stan Musial was the only non-Red voted to play in the July 9, 1957, game. As luck would have it, the American League edged the NL 6–5.

First manager to lose an All-Star game in both leagues

Sparky Anderson: National League, 1971, and American League, 1984

Surely, Sparky Anderson preferred being the first to manage World Series champions in both leagues, instead of being the first to manage All-Star losers in both leagues. Anderson was riding the wave of the Cincinnati Reds' 1970 World Series title when his National Leaguers fell 6–4 at Detroit's Tiger Stadium on July 13, 1971. Tiger Stadium was Anderson's home when the Tigers won the 1984 World Series. Then, on July 16, 1985, the AL suffered a 6–1 loss in the Hubert H. Humphrey Metrodome in Minneapolis.

Worst injury suffered during a team photo shoot— before an All-Star game

Broken nose: Cal Ripken Jr.

Cal Ripken Jr.'s consecutive-games-played streak almost got broken along with his nose when he suffered a freak injury during the American League team photo shoot before the All-Star game in Philadelphia, July 9, 1996. Pitcher Roberto Hernandez lost his balance, fell and, as he tried to regain his bearings, hit Ripken by accident in the nose. Ripken played despite his injury, but the

National League won 6–0. Ripken played a record 15 consecutive All-Star games for the AL.

Biggest musical instrument to "catch" an All-Star home-run ball

Tuba

Willie Stargell hit with a lot of oomph into oom-pa-pa territory on July 13, 1965. The Pittsburgh Pirates slugger slapped a two-run homer in the third inning at Metropolitan Stadium in Minneapolis, making it 5–0 for the National League. But the ball landed in a tuba just over the right-field wall where a band had been playing. The American League battled back for a 5–5 tie, which lasted until Willie Mays's seventh-inning, tie-breaking run for the NL.

Age of oldest All-Star game player

47: Satchel Paige, Cleveland

The oldest man on the diamond for the All-Star game on July 14, 1953, was Satchel Paige. The ageless wonder made his only appearance in the Midsummer Classic for the American League a week after he turned 47. Paige gave up two runs on three hits in a 5–1 loss to the National League.

Age of youngest All-Star game player

19: Dwight Gooden, New York (NL)

Dwight Gooden was baseball's teenage pitching sensation in 1984. Before he was voted the youngest Rookie of the Year, he was baseball's youngest All-Star. He was also the third of five National League pitchers in a 3–1 win on July 10, 1984, in San Francisco.

Most expensive tickets to an All-Star game tie

$175: Milwaukee, July 9, 2002

It cost $175 for a ticket to attend 2002's All-Star game in Milwaukee's

Miller Field. So how come many of the 41,871 fans chanted "Refund, refund, refund"? That's easy. The game was suspended in the 11th inning, tied 7–7, when the teams ran out of pitchers. All 60 players, including 10 National League pitchers and nine from the American League, saw action. The debacle of that draw led to the first meaningful game in All-Star history when, in 2003, the AL won 7–6 to gain home-field advantage in the World Series. The 2002 game wasn't the first tie in All-Star history, however. The leagues tied 1–1 on July 31, 1961, when a rainstorm prevented extra innings at Boston's Fenway Park.

CHAPTER 19

Hall of Fame, Hall of Shame

COOPERSTOWN OR BUST

Where do great baseball figures go when their careers are over? The Hall of Fame. Its hallowed halls are like heaven on earth for some fortunate ballplayers. For others, try as they might, there is just no getting through the gate. These players have their own place to go: the Hall of Shame.

First ballplayer honored league-wide

Harry Wright, April 13, 1896

When Harry Wright died of pneumonia on October 3, 1895, a pall fell over the National League as fans mourned the man who had guided baseball's first professional nine, the Cincinnati Red Stockings. And after raising $3,349 during games played in Wright's honor, they recognized the baseball great, on April 13, 1896, with a monument at West Laurel Hill Cemetery in Bala Cynwyd, Pennsylvania. Sadly, it took until 1953 for the Hall of Fame Veterans Committee to honor Wright with induction.

Most future Hall of Famers active in the same game

13: New York (AL) vs. Philadelphia, May 24, 1928

Thirteen was a lucky number for the fortunate Philadelphians who saw their Athletics host the New York Yankees in 1928. The teams featured 13 future members of baseball's Hall of Fame. Yankees Earle Combs, Leo Durocher, Babe Ruth, Lou Gehrig, Tony Lazzeri and Waite Hoyt opposed Athletics Ty Cobb, Tris Speaker, Mickey Cochrane, Al Simmons, Eddie Collins, Lefty Grove and Jimmie Foxx in the first game of a doubleheader. But that wasn't the end of the parade of greats. Fans also witnessed non-playing future Hall of Famers Herb Pennock, Stan Coveleski, Miller Huggins and Connie Mack, along with umpires Tom Connolly and Bill McGowan. New York won the opener 9–7; the A's took the nightcap 5–2.

Most national Hall of Fame memberships

4: Martin Dihigo

Call him El Maestro or El Immortal, but don't forget to call Martin Dihigo a member of four Halls of Fame. Although he never played in the majors, the legendary slugger and pitcher may be the most respected ballplayer in the Americas, inducted into

Halls of Fame in Cuba, Mexico, Venezuela and the United States. The Cuban native, who starred at every position except catcher, was honored by the Negro Leagues wing at Cooperstown in 1977.

Only Hall of Fame member born on a train
Rod Carew

Hall of Famer Rod Carew was born on a train in Gatun, Panama, on October 1, 1945. But that's not the way his mother planned it. She was heading to a hospital in Colon, Panama, when she went into labor; a doctor named Rodney delivered the baby. Carew was the American League's Rookie of the Year in 1967 and a 1991 Hall of Fame inductee after seven batting championships.

Cheapest seats named for a broadcaster recognized by the Hall of Fame
$1

Bob Uecker's six-year major league catching career took him to Milwaukee, Philadelphia, Atlanta and St. Louis—where he won the 1954 World Series with the Cardinals. But it was his work on radio and TV that earned him the Ford C. Frick Award for broadcasters, presented during the 2003 Hall of Fame induction ceremony. But for once, he was in the front row, unlike for TV's Miller Lite commercials, in which he was always up in the cheap seats. The part-time stand-up comedian, TV comedy star and Milwaukee Brewers longtime play-by-play announcer was honored by the cheapest seating category at Miller Field being named after him.

Cost of the biggest contract bonus gamble by a future Hall of Famer
$102,639.70: Warren Spahn, Atlanta

Warren Spahn joined the Hall of Fame in 1973 because of his talent as a lefty. But he also saved the Braves a lot of cash in 1953 when he left a six-figure bonus behind. Spahn could have earned 10 cents per ticket sold after the Boston Braves reached the 800,000-fan threshold. Instead, he took a $25,000 guarantee and scoffed at the commission offer, given that the Braves only attracted 300,000 fans per game in 1952. But when the Braves suddenly moved to Milwaukee in spring training in 1953, they drew 1,826,397 fans.

First $200,000-a-year player

Hank Aaron, Atlanta, February 29, 1972
Leap Year Day comes but once every four years, so Hank Aaron didn't let the opportunity to sign a big contract pass him by. The 1982 Hall of Fame inductee inked a $600,000, three-year deal with the Atlanta Braves on February 29, 1972, making him the first player with a $200,000-a-year contract.

Closest batting championship differential between Hall of Famers

0.000974: 1910
Baseball is a game of numbers—sometimes very, very small numbers. But on October 9, 1910, Ty Cobb snapped up the batting championship by a fraction when he batted .3850687 against rival Napoleon Lajoie's .3840947—a difference of 0.000974. Cobb was a charter member of the Hall of Fame in 1936; Lajoie was elected a year later.

First million-dollar holdout attempt

Sandy Koufax and Don Drysdale, 1966
Solidarity forever, or at least 32 days. On February 28, 1966, Los Angeles Dodgers pitchers Sandy Koufax and Don Drysdale announced that they were holding out for a joint three-year contract worth $1 million. Although on March 30, they signed one-year

deals for $130,000 and $110,000, respectively. Koufax was 36 when he became the youngest Hall of Fame inductee in 1972, after Lou Gehrig. Drysdale entered 12 years later.

Most Coca-Cola bottling plants owned by a Hall of Famer
3: Ty Cobb

Not until the 1980s did major league ballplayers hit the jackpot in terms of salaries and endorsements. For most of the century, players had to work in the off-season to make ends meet. But not Ty Cobb. Cobb, like Coca-Cola, hailed from Georgia, and both he and Coke were born in 1886. Cobb, who endorsed the soft drink in 1907 then bought 1,000 shares in 1918, purchased Coke bottling plants in California, Idaho and Oregon as he amassed a fortune estimated at more than $10 million before his death in 1961.

Most Hall of Fame votes cast for a banned player
41: Pete Rose, 1992

The Hall of Fame's voting committee kept his name off the ballot in 1992, but that didn't stop 41 members of the Baseball Writers Association of America from putting Pete Rose on their ballots. Still, pitchers Rollie Fingers and Tom Seaver were elected. Ten years later, there were still 18 die-hards offering their Rose votes, in part to protest baseball's ban of the all-time hit king for gambling on baseball while he managed the Reds. Rose eventually made it onto the 2003 ballot for Canada's Baseball Hall of Fame, but failed to get 75 per cent of selection committee votes. Finally, though he is not Canadian, Rose reached the 4,000-hit mark in 1985 with the Montreal Expos. In 2004, Rose finally admitted he bet on Reds games — after a decade and a half of denial.

Only Hall of Famer saved from drowning by a teammate
Frank Robinson, August 22, 1966
It was the greatest save by a non-pitcher away from a ballpark, when Baltimore Oriole catcher Andy Etchebarren rescued teammate Frank Robinson, a 1982 Hall of Famer, from drowning at a private party.

Only Hall of Famer cryogenically preserved
Ted Williams, 2002
They called him the Splendid Splinter, but in death he became a Popsicle. When Ted Williams died of cardiac arrest at age 83, on July 5, 2002, his son sent the Hall of Famer's body to Alcor Life Extension Foundation in Scottsdale, Arizona. The body and head were separated and preserved in a nitrogen-filled tank—an experimental process called cryogenics that predicts science will one day be able to resurrect or clone dead humans. Williams's daughter, however, claimed her father wanted his cremated ashes scattered off the Florida coast. But her siblings said they had agreed with Ted in 2000 to send their own bodies to a cryogenics lab. Williams's daughter finally gave up her legal fight in December 2002, when a judge agreed to distribute the $645,000 trust fund among the three children. The remainder of the fortune will be doled out in 2012.

CHAPTER 20

Legends of the Fall

LEAGUE CHAOS AND

WORLD SERIOUS

Spring is long gone and summer's memories are fading, as the days get shorter and the nights longer. The chill brings with it falling leaves and even a hint of frost. Meanwhile, two teams are rising above the rest, with their collective eyes fixed on the prize: the World Series.

First single-city World Series

1906: Chicago

The Chicago Cubs won a record 116 games for the 1906 National League pennant, with a 20-game advantage over the runner-up New York Giants. It all started when the Chicago White Sox slipped past the New York Yankees with a three-game cushion in the American League. This set up the first single-city World Series, and it was a shocker. The cocky Cubs were upset in six games by the White Sox, nicknamed the Hitless Wonders. The Sox rapped 11 hits in the first four games then exploded with 26 in the final two to clinch the title. Still, the Yankees are the king of single-city World Series, winning 11 times and losing five without leaving the Big Apple.

Most consecutive times a team was eliminated from the playoffs by the same team

3: Kansas City by New York (AL), 1976, 1977 and 1978

It was routine for the New York Yankees to beat the Kansas City Royals in the American League championship during the 1970s. In fact, the Yankees disappointed the Royals three straight seasons. The first time was in 1976, as the Yankees defeated the Royals in the fifth game of the ALCS on Chris Chambliss's series-winning home run in the bottom of the ninth at Yankee Stadium. The Royals wanted revenge, but they didn't get it in 1977: the Yankees won the deciding fifth game in Kansas City. Finally, on October 4, 1978, the Yankees got their hat trick over the Royals. But this time they wrapped it up in Game 4 with a 2–1 win, thanks to home runs by Graig Nettles and Roy White.

First World Series in which the home team won all games

Minnesota vs. St. Louis, 1987

The Minnesota Twins have never lost a World Series game at their dome, but during their 1987 and 1991 championship seasons, they lost all their road games in the Fall Classic. It was a good thing they had home-field advantage. They beat the St. Louis Cardinals in 1987 and the Atlanta Braves in 1991, both times by winning the seventh game at the Hubert H. Humphrey Metrodome. The Arizona Diamondbacks, who beat the New York Yankees in 2001, are the only other team to equal the Twins' feat. In 1920, the Cleveland Indians were the first team to win four World Series home games when they beat the Brooklyn Robins 5–2 in a best-of-nine series.

Most World Series championships for a player
10: Yogi Berra, New York (AL)
New York Yankees catching great Yogi Berra has a World Series ring for every finger. He played in 14 Fall Classics, the most of any player in history. Berra's first was in 1947, when the Yankees beat the crosstown rival Brooklyn Dodgers in seven games. His last was in 1962, against the San Francisco Giants.

Most World Series won by a non-American-based team
2: Toronto, 1992 and 1993
Another American tradition came to an end on October 24, 1992, when a non-American team won the World Series. Canada's Toronto Blue Jays won their first of two consecutive titles with a Game 6 victory over the host Atlanta Braves in 1992. The Jays repeated the feat in 1993, at home against the Philadelphia Phillies.

Most consecutive World Series championships
5: New York (AL), 1949 to 1953
The New York Yankees of 1949 to 1953 are considered among the best teams in baseball history. Why? They won the World Series every season during that time span, during which they went 20–8 against National League champs. Some fans, however, say

the 1936 to 1939 Yankees were better, despite the fact they won one fewer World Series titles. A four- or five-championship dynasty today would be an even bigger achievement, because the World Series no longer begins immediately after the regular season ends. Teams must win a best-of-five division championship and best-of-seven league championship before they can even think about winning the World Series.

Most managers to share an apartment during a World Series

2: Luke Sewell and Billy Southworth, 1944

In 1944, the St. Louis Cardinals beat the St. Louis Browns in six games at Sportsman's Park in the Missouri city. But not only did the teams share a stadium and city, Browns manager Luke Sewell shared an apartment with the Cardinals' skipper, Billy Southworth. The Browns were 89–65 in the American League regular season; the Cardinals repeated as National League winners with a 105–49 record.

Most money donated to charity after a World Series tie game

$120,554: 1922

Umpire George Hildebrand didn't earn any praise from fans of either the New York Yankees or the New York Giants when the teams were tied 3–3 in Game 2 of the World Series on October 5, 1922. At 4:45 PM, Hildebrand stopped the game due to the failing light, and the World Series had its first tie. Hildebrand may have been the only person at the Polo Grounds who thought it was too dim to continue—sunset was at least one hour away. Angry fans flooded the field in protest, hoping for refunds. Instead, Commissioner Kenesaw Mountain Landis ordered that the $120,554 gate revenue for the game be donated to charity.

Longest World Series home-run drought

23 games: 1903 to 1908

When Boston Pilgrim Patsy Dougherty hit a pair of home runs in the second game of 1903's World Series on October 2, 1903, they were the last seen in the Fall Classic until 1908. Chicago Cub Joe Tinker hit one in Game 2 on October 11, 1908, as the Cubs beat the Detroit Tigers 6–1 en route to a five-game championship.

Most legendary World Series home run

Babe Ruth's "called shot," October 1, 1932

When Babe Ruth stepped to the plate in the fifth inning at Wrigley Field in Chicago during Game 3 of the World Series, he responded to the jeers of Cubs fans by pointing to the outfield wall. Ruth then sent a 2–2 pitch from hurler Charlie Root into the center-field bleachers. Baseball historians often debate whether he was mocking fans or just pointing out the spot where he would send the ball. The home run, forever known as Ruth's "called shot," broke a 4–4 tie and keyed the Yankees' 7–5 win.

Most home runs in a postseason game by a ninth-spot batter

3: Adam Kennedy, Anaheim, 2002

Adam Kennedy liked being in last place. The Anaheim Angel had three homers in Game 5 of the 2002 American League championship while batting ninth. His blasts sparked a 13–5 Angels victory over the Minnesota Twins.

Biggest tie-breaking World Series-winning home run

Bill Mazeroski, Pittsburgh, 1960

It couldn't get any better than this for Pittsburgh Pirates fans on October 13, 1960. Bottom of the ninth, Game 7 of the World Series, and Bill Mazeroski comes to the plate with the score tied

9–9. What does he do? He hits a home run—the biggest tie-break-ing, winning homer of any World Series— to complete a stunning upset of the heavily favored New York Yankees.

Most historic firsts in a World Series game, post-1903

3: *first grand slam, first home run by a pitcher and first unassisted triple play, Cleveland, October 10, 1920*

The fifth game of the 1920 World Series was a day for firsts. Not since the first World Series in 1903 had so many statistical mile-stones been reached on one day. Cleveland Indian second base-man Bill Wambsganss, the hometown boy, registered the first unassisted triple play when he ended the fifth inning by grabbing Clarence Mitchell's line drive, catching Pete Kilduff at second and tagging Otto Miller on the baseline. Wambsganss was also one of three men on base in the first inning when Elmer Smith hit the first World Series grand slam. Jim Bagby, who went the dis-tance on the Indians mound, hit a three-run homer in the fourth off Brooklyn starter Burleigh Grimes. Brooklyn never recovered. They lost the game 8–1 and the series five games to two.

Most runs and hits by one team in a postseason game

23 runs and 24 hits: October 10, 1999

It wasn't the New England Patriots and the Cleveland Browns, but the score looked like one from the gridiron when the Boston Red Sox beat the Cleveland Indians 23–7 at Fenway Park in Boston, in Game 4 of the American League Division series. The Red Sox registered a record 24 hits. The teams' combined 30 runs were also a record for two teams in postseason play. The next night, the Red Sox finished off the Indians with a 12–8 win at Cleveland.

Most runs in a postseason series

82: New York vs. Pittsburgh, 1960

The 1960 World Series between the Pittsburgh Pirates and New York Yankees kept the scorekeepers busy. The Yankees outscored the Pirates 55–27 in seven games to become the highest-scoring World Series losers in history.

First player to bat first and last in both the league championship and World Series

Kenny Lofton, San Francisco, 2002

Kenny Lofton was the first and last batter of the league championship and World Series in 2002. But that's little reward for a man whose San Francisco Giants lost the World Series. Lofton walked to begin Game 1 of the National League championship between his Giants and the St. Louis Cardinals. His ninth inning RBI single on October 14, 2002, won the pennant. Lofton again batted first and last in the World Series.

Most future managers on the same team hit by pitches in a World Series game

3: Davey Johnson, Frank Robinson and Andy Etchebarren, Baltimore, October 13, 1971

Pirates reliever Bruce Kison hit three Orioles batters during the first World Series night game in 1971 — Davey Johnson, Frank Robinson and Andy Etchebarren — as he pitched 6⅓ innings, beating the Orioles 4–3 at Three Rivers Stadium. (Pittsburgh eventually won the World Series in seven games.) Coincidentally, all three "hit men" went on to manage professionally after their playing days were over. Johnson and Robinson skippered teams in the majors, while Etchebarren was a dugout boss in class AAA and a first-base coach and bench coach in the majors.

Most saves in a World Series

4: John Wetteland, New York (AL), 1996

New York Yankees reliever John Wetteland proved that defense wins championships when he recorded four saves in just $4^{1}/_{3}$ innings of five World Series games in 1996. Wetteland was subsequently named Most Valuable Player.

Most pitchers named Blue in the same playoff victory

2: Blue Moon Odom and Vida Blue, Oakland, October 12, 1972

Oakland Athletics pitchers Blue Moon Odom and Vida Blue weren't singing the blues in the 1972 World Series, when they combined for a 2–1 American League championship series-ending victory over the Detroit Tigers. Odom—born Johnny Lee Odom— had the win, and Blue (a sixth-inning reliever) had the save.

Most World Series wins over three decades

3: Jim Palmer, Baltimore

Baltimore Orioles ace pitcher Jim Palmer stood the test of time. He pitched his team to World Series game victories in the '60s, '70s and '80s. His first was in Game 2 of the 1966 championship against the Los Angeles Dodgers, a 6–0 win. Then in Game 2 of the 1971 series with the Pittsburgh Pirates, on October 11, Palmer was an 11–3 winner. His last came on October 14, 1983, a 3–2 win over the Philadelphia Phillies in Game 3.

Most playoff wins before winning a regular-season game

4: Francisco Rodriguez, Anaheim, October 10, 2002

Francisco Rodriguez not only won four playoff games before he won a regular-season game, he was the second pitcher to lose a

World Series game before losing one in the regular season. The Anaheim Angels pitcher beat Felix Rodriguez (no relation) of the Giants 11–10 in Game 2 and appeared in 5⅔ innings of action during five regular-season games. He started none of them, but he did finish four.

Only World Series-winning pitcher to become another team's doctor
Ron Taylor
Ron Taylor never got a chance to play big league ball in his hometown, but he did get to practise for the home team as its doctor. Taylor was born in Toronto and tasted World Series success with the 1964 St. Louis Cardinals and 1969 New York Mets. When his playing days were over, he became the Toronto Blue Jays' team physician in February 1979. Taylor actually studied electrical engineering while he was playing baseball, but returned to the University of Toronto's medical school after his 1972 retirement from the game.

Most disgruntled World Series-winning team
1973 Oakland Athletics
It was the classic carrot on the stick, though in this case, you could say it was Charlie Finley's carat-less schtick. When they won the 1972 World Series, owner Finley promised the Oakland Athletics bigger and better championship rings if they repeated in 1973. (The players had been presented with one-carat diamond rings for their 1972 championship.) But in 1973, after again winning the series, their rings contained only a synthetic emerald—and no diamond.

Longest pigeon delay in World Series history
5 minutes: Washington, D.C., October 5, 1933
Had the Washington Senators used the momentum of their

Game 3 victory in the 1933 World Series, "pigeon power" would have been all the rage. A pigeon that refused to leave the field caused a five-minute delay when Washington hosted the New York Giants on October 5, 1933. But although the Senators were 4–0 winners of the game, they lost the next two and the series.

First burial of an American League pennant
Cleveland, September 23, 1949
It was painfully clear that the 1948 World Series champion Cleveland Indians would not repeat in 1949. So the day after they were eliminated from playoff contention, owner Bill Veeck staged a mock funeral at Municipal Stadium for the 1948 pennant. Manager Lou Boudreau and his coaches laid the flag to rest, acting as pallbearers of a pine coffin that was planted behind the outfield wall. The atmosphere remained downbeat when the Detroit Tigers blanked the Indians 5–0.

Biggest fine for an owner trying to demote a player during a World Series
$5,000: Charlie Finley, Oakland, October 15, 1973
Oakland Athletics owner Charlie Finley was livid when second baseman Mike Andrews made back-to-back 12th-inning errors. The mistakes allowed the New York Mets to score four runs, then rally to win the second game of the 1973 World Series 10–7 on October 14. As a result, Finley wanted Andrews demoted to the disabled list for the remainder of the series. But when major league commissioner Bowie Kuhn found out about Finley's finagling, he slapped him with a $5,000 fine. Although that didn't stop Finley from later releasing Andrews, who retired from baseball with a World Series title when the Athletics beat the Yankees in seven games.

Age of youngest player in a World Series

18: Fred Lindstrom, New York (NL)

New York Giants third baseman Fred Lindstrom wanted an early 19th birthday present: the World Series. The Giants were 4–3 winners in Lindstrom's first World Series game on October 4, 1924, against the Washington Senators, but the Senators were winners of the title in seven games. Lindstrom was born November 21, 1905.

Age of oldest pitcher to start and finish a World Series game

46: Jack Quinn, Philadelphia (AL)

When Philadelphia Athletics pitcher Jack Quinn played Game 3 of the 1930 World Series against the St. Louis Cardinals, he was the oldest player on the field. And he's still the most senior World Series competitor. (The Athletics were 5–0 winners of the game and 4–2 winners of the series.) Quinn, born July 5, 1883, is also the oldest player to hit a home run.

Age of oldest manager to win a World Series

72: Jack McKeon

Most people in their seventies who go to Florida are there on holiday or to retire. But not Jack McKeon, who in May 2003 came out of retirement in Burlington, North Carolina, to work as the Florida Marlins manager, then guided them to their second World Series championship. McKeon grew up in New Jersey, across the Hudson River from Yankee Stadium, where he finally won the championship on October 25, 2003. (The only other manager to take over midseason and win a World Series was 1978 New York Yankees bench boss Bob Lemon.)

Most seasons played without a World Series appearance

24: Phil Niekro

Pity poor Phil Niekro. He played 24 years in the major leagues without ever appearing on the mound in a World Series game. The closest he came was with Atlanta in the National League championship series of 1969 and 1982. The New York Mets swept the Braves in three games in 1969, then the St. Louis Cardinals did the same in 1982—beating the Braves en route to winning the World Series both times. Phil Niekro's younger brother, Joe, played 22 seasons, and won the World Series with the 1987 Minnesota Twins.

Coldest World Series game

15 degrees Fahrenheit: Cleveland, October 22, 1997

The Florida Marlins weren't accustomed to chilly temperatures, which might explain their Game 4 loss during the 1997 World Series when the Cleveland Indians beat the Marlins 10–3 in the 15-degree cold. The Marlins rebounded, however, and won the World Series at home on Edgar Renteria's bases-loaded single in the bottom of the 11th inning of October 26's Game 7.

Most flags on a professional sports championship trophy

30: Major League Baseball Commissioner's Trophy

The trophy presented to the winner of the World Series contains one flag for each of the 30 big league teams. Made by New York City's Tiffany and Co., the 24-inch-high and 11-inch-diameter trophy also contains longitude and latitude lines and 24-karat vermeil stitches, just like on a baseball. It also contains 198.12 troy ounces of sterling silver, valued at $15,000. But for the team that wins it, the Commissioner's Trophy is priceless.

Most teams played on in a World Series career

4: Lonnie Smith, Philadelphia (NL), St. Louis (NL), Kansas City and Atlanta

Some players are lucky to play in one World Series, but Lonnie Smith played in five—with four different teams. Smith, a veteran outfielder born in Chicago, won World Series rings with the 1980 Philadelphia Phillies, 1982 St. Louis Cardinals and 1985 Kansas City Royals, but was on the losing end with the Atlanta Braves in 1991 and 1992.

First pitcher caught scalping tickets to his team's World Series games

Rube Marquard, Brooklyn, October 9, 1920

An undercover policeman busted Brooklyn Dodgers pitcher Rube Marquard for flogging eight World Series box seats before Game 4 of the 1920 classic. The face value of the four tickets was $52.80, though Marquard's asking price was $400. He was fined $1 plus $2.80 for court costs. But that wasn't all Marquard lost. He was a 3–1 victim of the Indians in Game 1 on October 5.

Most shutout wins by a pitcher who sat out a World Series opener for religious reasons

2: Sandy Koufax, October 6, 1965

Sandy Koufax put his Jewish faith ahead of baseball when he decided not to pitch in the opening game against the Minnesota Twins on October 6, 1965. The date coincided with Yom Kippur, the holiest of Jewish holidays. Koufax's start was delayed to Game 2, which the Dodgers lost 5–1. Koufax was there when it mattered the most, however, leading the Dodgers to a 7–0 shutout win in

Game 5 on October 11 and a 2–0 whitewash on October 14 in the deciding seventh game.

Largest crowd to attend a postseason game

92,706: Los Angeles, October 6, 1959

When the World Series came to the west coast, Los Angelinos wanted to know what all the fuss was about: Game 5 of the 1959 World Series attracted a record 92,706 fans. Part of the reason there were so many people was the size of Los Angeles Memorial Coliseum, where the Dodgers played until their own stadium was built. The Chicago White Sox shocked the mammoth crowd with a 1–0 win, but the Dodgers got revenge in Chicago on October 8, where they won the series.

Smallest attendance for a World Series game

6,210: Detroit, October 14, 1908

Only 6,210 people cared to show up for the Chicago Cubs' 2–0 series-clinching Game 5 win over the Detroit Tigers in Detroit. Apparently, Tigers fans gave up on hopes that their team might make a miracle comeback.

First prime time World Series telecast

October 13, 1971: Pittsburgh vs. Baltimore

An estimated 61 million people watched NBC's coverage of the Pittsburgh Pirates' 4–3 win over the Baltimore Orioles in the fourth game of the 1971 World Series—the first played during the east coast's prime time TV schedule.

Biggest Richter scale measurement for a World Series-delaying earthquake

7.1: San Francisco vs. Oakland, 1989

The earth moved when the World Series moved across the bay to

San Francisco's Candlestick Park on October 17, 1989, when seismologists measured an earthquake at 7.1 on the Richter scale in northern California. Game 3 of the World Series was postponed until October 27, but the favored Oakland Athletics shook no one when they won it in a four-game sweep.

Most players from the same team banned for gambling

8: George "Buck" Weaver, Eddie Cicotte, Joe Jackson, Arnold "Chick" Gandil, Charles "Swede" Risberg, Claude "Lefty" Williams, Oscar "Happy" Felsch and Fred McMullin, Chicago (AL)

They are forever known as the "eight men out"—the Chicago White Sox who conspired with a trio of Boston gamblers to lose the best-of-nine 1919 World Series to the longshot Cincinnati Reds. The eight players received a total of $80,000 for their lack of effort, though ringleader "Chick" Gandil scooped $35,000 of the sum. The players, who faced five years in jail and $10,000 in fines if found guilty, were acquitted on August 2, 1921. That didn't stop Commissioner Kenesaw Mountain Landis from banning them from the game, however. "Regardless of the verdicts of juries, baseball is entirely competent to protect itself against the crooks, both inside and outside the game," he said.

Most presumptuous major media outlet

New York Post, 2003

The editorial writers at the *New York Post* wrote off the hometown Yankees too early during the 2003 American League championship finale, so they could meet their press deadline for the October 17 edition. "The hitting fell short and the bullpen simply didn't deliver... the World Series should be one helluva series—even without the Yanks," it said. But Aaron Boone's 11th-inning home run and reliever Mariano Riviera's relief pitching gave the Yankees the pennant and the *Post*'s editor a red face.

Acknowledgements

Thanks to the following for the use of statistical material:

- *Total Baseball: The Official Encyclopedia of Major League Baseball,* 7th edition (Total Sports)
- *Baseball: The Biographical Encyclopedia* (Total Sports)
- *Official Major League Baseball Fact Book,* 2003 edition (Sporting News)
- *The Cultural Encyclopedia of Baseball* by Jonathan Fraser Light (McFarland)
- *The Baseball Timeline* by Burt Solomon (DK Publishing)
- *Baseball Extra* (Castle)
- *www.retrosheet.org*
- *Record-Breaking Baseball Trivia* by Bob Mackin (Greystone)
- *Off the Wall Baseball Trivia* by Bob Mackin (Greystone)
- Numerous team media guides

The author also gratefully acknowledges the help of Rob Sanders, Susan Rana, Anne Rose, Kerry Banks, Peter Cocking, Tanya Lloyd Kyi, Jessica Sullivan, Viola Funk, Chris Labonte and the rest at Greystone; Kit Krieger, Max Weder, Colin Preston, Alfie Lau, Pat Karl, Jay and Irene Berman, Mick Maloney, Neville Judd, Jason Rowland, Jonathan Mackin, Society for American Baseball Research members—and baseball fans everywhere. As well, the author gives special thanks the staff of the National Baseball Library & A. Bartlett Giamatti Research Center and Vancouver Public Library sports reference department.

Index